Raising
the Next Generation

Raising the Next Generation

Stories from the Past, Applied to the Present, Shape the Future

Volume 1

Chuck Clifton

Writers Club Press
San Jose New York Lincoln Shanghai

Raising the Next Generation
Stories from the Past, Applied to the Present, Shape the Future

Writers Club Press
an imprint of iUniverse, Inc.

For information address:
iUniverse, Inc.
5220 S. 16th St., Suite 200
Lincoln, NE 68512
www.iuniverse.com

This book has descritpions of ideas that have worked in the raising of some children. This in no way implies that these methods will work for anyone else.

ISBN: 0-595-22329-X

Printed in the United States of America

This book is dedicated to all the children of future generations, wherever or whenever they may be born. May your experience on this earth be better because of those who have dedicated their lives to do the best jobs they can at Raising the Next Generation.

CONTENTS

LIST OF ILLUSTRATIONS

Front Cover Photo of Trevor and Ethan Clifton, July 23, 2001 taken by Tanya Bingham

All of the following photographs are from the Chuck Clifton Family Collection

PREFACE

This book, as its title suggests, is a book about raising children. It is the first in a series of books that will offer parents and grandparents ways in which they can play a positive role in providing good experiences for children as they progress through life. It can be read from cover to cover or used as a reference guide to provide assistance and encouragement.

Volume One contains more than 100 true stories that are about the experiences we've had while raising our children. These experiences reflect the parenting strategies that we have used over the years. Some worked very well; others have not. Some worked with a few of the children, but not with others. We include them all because they have been valuable to us in one way or another. Our family is far from perfect, and we have had our share of failures along with the successes. However, one theme that underlies our efforts is that, as parents, we have never stopped trying—even when times got tough. We found that the tougher things got, the more creative and determined we needed to be.

This volume also contains a glossary in Appendix D. It is included as an aide to understanding some words and phrases we have used that might be unfamiliar to you. Quite often, these pertain to special things we have, or things we do, in our home. The first time each of these words or phrases is mentioned in the text, it will be followed by "see glossary" in parentheses.

This book has the complete endorsement of my trusted companion of nearly three decades: my wife, Joyce. Without her, these stories would not have happened. Without her permission, they never would have been published. She has been a major factor in almost every story told here. Sometimes she just turned her head and let me try something, but usually, she dove in and fully participated. I have always felt her complete support in all that we have done as a family.

It is with mixed emotions that we share this intimate look inside our lives. However, each day, we encounter many parents who seem unaware of the joy that being a parent can bring. They get frustrated and confused when trying to raise a family in today's society. So, it is with love for children everywhere that we share our successful techniques, our personal beliefs, and the precious experiences we've had while raising our own children. We do so with the hope that you can gain some insight into how to bring more happiness into your own home as you go about "Raising the Next Generation."

We Want to Hear Your Stories

We realize that not all families have the same structure, environment, or belief system that ours does. Therefore, future volumes of *Raising the Next Generation* will contain collections of *positive* stories from readers like you. You may submit your true stories on our web site at: www.RaisingNextGeneration.com.

Your impact on future generations is already twofold: you are raising your own children, and you are influencing how your children raise their families. By sharing your positive, insightful stories, you will be impacting future generations in yet a third way: you will be offering successful parenting strategies and styles to a multitude of others. So, whatever your family situation is, we are anxious to hear from you.

ACKNOWLEDGEMENTS

I would like to thank all of those who made this book and its accompanying web site possible. I appreciate all of the effort put forth by those who have reviewed various forms of the manuscript and for their timely feedback. This list includes Brenda Beutler, Alvin Sebastien, Jeff Hill, Scottia Reidhead, Kathleen Higgins, Mary Haymore, and Robert and Cary Mumme. I would also like to thank Stephanie Holt at Online Freelance Editor for her professional work in taking my rough manuscript and turning it into something readable.

I thank my children as well for reviewing the content of this book, and for letting me "practice" on them as I have learned about Raising the Next Generation. They are, from youngest to oldest, Shayla Clifton, Capri Clifton, Dacia Clifton, Trent Clifton, Blake Clifton, Tanya Bingham, Monica Clifton, Carmin Clifton, Trevor Clifton, and Dionne Squires. My best reviewer, however, has been my patient wife, Joyce Clifton. Her method of toning me down is especially appreciated.

I especially thank all of those parents who have crossed my path and taught me about parenting. This includes my parents-in-law, Oakley and Janet Ray, for the fine way in which they have answered the call of being parents and for the way in which they have raised their daughter, who now wears my last name. It also includes my own parents, the late Chuck Clifton Sr. and Dot Clifton, for giving me a chance to grow up in a home full of love and for instilling in me, from the beginning, the desire to raise my own family.

Most of all, I am thankful to my wife, Joyce, who has been with me every step of the way as we have progressed from newlyweds, to first-time parents, to parents of ten children, to grandparents.

INTRODUCTION

Being a parent is a fulltime job. Even though it takes many sacrifices, it can be very rewarding. The most important thing to keep in mind is that you are responsible for raising members of the next generation. You will play a major role in how your children turn out. They, in turn, will play major roles in how the succeeding generation will turn out, and so on. It is impossible to measure how important your impact on a single child will be to the future generations of the human race. You are special!

Most people think that a full-time job consists of putting in 40 hours per week, with occasional sick days, vacation days and holidays. This may be true in the workplace, but at home, your job as a parent consists of 168 hours each and every week—with no sick time, vacation days or holidays off. There is only one shift for parenting: all day and all night.

At work, you are paid wages and awarded benefits for your 40 hours. Before you receive this compensation, there are various government entities that get their fair share via state and federal taxes. In other words, all of the compensation you earn does not make it into your bank. As a parent, however, you are compensated for your 168 hours with blessings. These come to you night and day, and they will last a lifetime, long after any money you may have earned at work has been spent. Also, all of the blessings that you are rewarded with are untouched by governments. The entire reward is yours to keep forever.

At your job, you work until you reach the age of retirement, usually 65 years of age. Then, you join the ranks of the retired—those who do not need to worry about their careers anymore. Your job as a parent, however, never ends. You are a parent for as long as you live. Even though your children grow up, move out, and begin raising families of their own—you will continue to have a profound influence on them. Perhaps your day-to-day duties concerning them will significantly decrease, but when they *do* need your help, it will be important for you to be there.

Parenting is obviously not an easy undertaking, but it can be incredibly fun and rewarding! Just like any job in the workplace, what you get out of parenting depends on what you put into it. In our home, we have made parenting the highest priority, and we feel that we have been richly rewarded for doing so.

Our Family

Since the stories in this book are based on the members of our family, we would like to take this opportunity to introduce them to you:

Chuck is the Dad. The best thing that I ever did in life was to marry Joyce. I have a BS in Math and an MS in Computer Science. My employment consists of being a Software Consultant, but my fulltime job is being a Dad.

Joyce is the mother of our ten children. She also operates a small baking business out of our home with the kids' help. Joyce has a BS in Education and she is fluent in Spanish.

Dionne is daughter #1. She is married to Matt and they have two sons, Connor and Spencer. Matt is pursuing his PhD in Physics. Dionne has a BS in Education and is fluent in American Sign Language. Matt is fluent in Spanish.

Trevor is son #1. He is married to Amy and they have one son named Ethan. Trevor has a BS in Computer Science and Amy has a BS in Family Science. Trevor is employed as a Software Engineer. Both Trevor and Amy are fluent in Italian. Trevor is an Eagle Scout with five Eagle Palms.

Carmin is daughter #2. She has a BS in Family Science. She currently works as a Conference Coordinator at the Aspen Grove Family Conference Center near Sundance, Utah. She is fluent in Romanian.

Monica is daughter #3. She has a BS in Education and is a qualified Lifeguard and Medical Assistant. She currently works as a medical assistant.

Tanya is daughter #4. She is married to Logan. They lost the first of their daughters, Mackenzie, at birth. Their second daughter, Janessa was born two months early. She is now home and doing well after a lengthy hospital stay. Tanya is pursuing a degree in Family Science and Logan is pursuing a degree in Construction Management. Logan is fluent in Vietnamese.

Blake is son #2. He is currently serving a mission (see glossary) in Japan for our church. He completed one year of pre-med classes before he left. He is fluent in Japanese and is an Eagle Scout with five Eagle Palms.

Trent is son #3. He is in high school and is a member of the Utah County Explorer Search and Rescue team. He enjoys carving chainsaw bears and making lodge pole pine furniture. Trent knows American Sign Language and he is an Eagle Scout with nine Eagle Palms.

Dacia is daughter #5. She has just become a teenager. She has a great sense of humor, even when the joke is on her. At age two, she hiked 4½ miles down into the Grand Canyon and another 4½ miles back to the top. She did it without complaint and even skipped the last 100 yards!

Capri is daughter #6. She is eleven and is very athletic. She loves animals, especially horses. At the age of three, she rode a two-wheeled bicycle without training wheels, unassisted, down the street.

Shayla is daughter #7. She is the youngest and now attends school all day. Aside from Joyce and me, Shayla, being the youngest, has nine other "parents." She does well, despite this fact.

Chapter 1—Bonding

Bonding is a word that may be somewhat overused in our society today. However, there is no such thing as too much bonding between a parent and a child. It comes in many different forms, as illustrated in the following stories. However, bonding between a parent and their child is very important, and it can (and should) occur with kids at all ages, throughout their lives. Children can also bond with siblings, grandparents, other family members, and even close friends—but nothing can replace establishing a long-lasting bond between a parent and child.

The stories in this chapter reflect some of the experiences that we have had while bonding with our children. We are always looking for new ways to bond with them, so we are always trying to learn from others.

Reading to Children

Joyce has made it a habit to read to our children almost every night, and this has provided a strong bond between them that could not have been achieved any other way. We have collected various books of the children's classics over the years, and they have paid big dividends several times over.

Sometimes, when Joyce is reading to the younger children, one of the older kids will walk past the room, stop, and sit awhile to listen again to a favorite story they heard many times when they were young.

When Shayla was three years old, I worked at home. Whenever she asked me to read her a story, I always dropped what I was doing and obliged. She learned the names of many animals and many famous places by seeing their pictures in the books I read to her. Those reading sessions not only provided a chance for Shayla and me to bond, but they also served as a fun educational tool.

Wanna Play Old Maid?

For her third birthday, Shayla got a deck of Old Maid cards. She would carry them around the house asking everyone, "Wanna play Old Maid?" Usually, she found one of her older siblings to play. However, on school days, the other kids would be gone. Joyce was usually busy and I was usually in my office, writing software or on the phone with a client.

One day, my office door slowly opened and a tiny hand holding a ragged box of Old Maid cards wiggled through the crack. Then, a soft voice said, "Wanna play Old Maid?" I quickly finished what I was doing and said, "Yes, I wanna play Old Maid!" The door flew open and she ran into the office, plopped down on the floor, and immediately began dealing the cards. I joined her and we had lots of fun. A game only lasted about five minutes, but the memory will last a lifetime.

Aside from being a fun experience for both of us, it provided me an opportunity to teach Shayla one-on-one. After playing several games with her over the next few days, I noticed that I was always dealt the Old Maid. Without accusing her of cheating, we merely had a nice talk about honesty and being fair. After that, I only got the Old Maid about 50% of the time. According to modern statistics theory, that is to be expected. I was able to teach a simple principle to her at an early age— one that will hopefully pave the way for a better life.

The Swim Team and Duct Tape

One year, Trent invited the entire high school swim team over to our home for their annual party. They came in droves with stacks of pizza boxes. We have always tried to get involved in our kids' activities with their friends. But the swim team members were, for the most part, unknown to us.

As the party progressed, the kids played pool, Ping Pong, and the piano. Then, I noticed a few guys trying to secretly pass around a roll of Duct Tape. All at once, they grabbed a young swimmer, bent him into a pretzel shape, taped him up, and left him squirming on the floor. The prank caught Trent by surprise, and he wasn't sure how I would react. For the time being, I just turned my head.

A little later, I saw the pranksters standing in a small circle, obviously making plans for their next victim. I walked over to them and they immediately hid the tape, afraid that they were in trouble. I told them that I had a great idea. They listened intently as I explained that I wanted them to tape *me* up—but that I didn't want them to let anyone know, especially Trent, that it was my idea.

I then wandered around a bit and finally sat down next to some young ladies and struck up a conversation with them. The guys slowly drifted into the room and gathered around me. All of a sudden, one of them yelled, "Let's tape up Mr. Clifton!"

The big ones grabbed me and held me while the others taped me up. I pretended to struggle. I wanted to see what Trent would do…and he did the right thing: he grabbed the digital camera.

Soon, I was twisted, contorted, and covered in Duct Tape! It covered my legs, ankles, wrists, arms and knees. When the boys were finished, everyone just stared at me, wondering if I would be angry. I, of course, acted very surprised that they had done this to me. I struggled to get free, and soon, all of the lady swimmers were at my side offering sympathy. Quickly, they helped remove the tape. And they did a fine job too—except for that one strip around my wrist that, when removed, took a large patch of hair with it. It took months to grow back.

Meanwhile, Trent took some great pictures. Those guys kept their secret and became good pals of mine. The young ladies treated me so well and were so helpful that I became their friend as well. Six months passed before I told Trent that I had put the guys up to that trick. We have laughed about it many times since. It was worth every second of the torture. You should always get to know your kids' friends—at all costs.

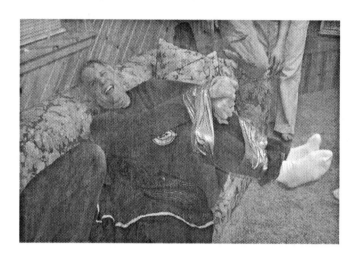

Photo # 1: Chuck was taped up with duct tape by the swim team.

A Surprise Vacation

Of all the vacations that we have ever gone on, the one that was perhaps the most fun was one in which I did not tell anyone, not even Joyce, where we were going or what we would be doing. I told them that we would leave on Monday, July 13, 1992 at 6:00 AM. I told them that we would return no later than midnight on Saturday, July 18, 1992. I gave them a few clues, but didn't reveal any details. They had no idea what to expect.

About a month prior to the trip, I finalized my plan. I had requested information from Yosemite National Park, San Diego, Lake Powell, Zion National Park, Bryce Canyon, Grand Canyon, Yellowstone, Grand

Tetons, Durango Colorado, Rocky Mountain National Park and a few other places. I told the family that we were going on a trip, and that they would not know where we were going until we got there. Each day, when the brochures arrived in the mail, Joyce and the kids would make new guesses as to where we were going.

I then gave them a few clues by providing a list of every meal that we would eat while on vacation. This included Wednesday's meal of bean burritos and macaroni and cheese. They all figured out that on that night, I would not be eating with them, since I don't like either one. So, they surmised that Joyce and I would be eating out that night. Other clues were hidden in the names and descriptions of the other meals. The food consisted of such things as "Texas" burgers, "Sub" sandwiches, and "Caesar" Salad. Some clues, however, were intended as decoys.

I gave each person a checklist of things to pack for the trip and I made a general six-page list of family items that we would need to take. It included ocean going gear, like swim suits, boogie boards and beach towels; cold weather things, like wool blankets, sweatshirts and sock hats; and camping and fishing gear. The list also included books, maps, and information on various attractions in several surrounding states.

Soon, it became a contest to see who could correctly guess where we were going. Many of our friends even got involved. Several men wanted me to secretly tell them where we were going, but my lips remained sealed!

Dionne couldn't go with us that year because she was committed to her office job at a trucking company. Still, about half of the workers in her office were trying to figure out the clues. I promised Dionne that when we arrived at our destination, I would call her and tell her where we were and what we would be doing for the week. I left her a sealed envelope with some money and a note that suggested she should take a friend out to dinner on Wednesday night. But she was not to open the envelope until Wednesday. In a small way, it helped to include her in our vacation plans.

When the day of our departure finally arrived, excitement was in the air! I have never had an easier time getting the kids up and ready to leave on a Monday morning. We actually left our Peoria, Arizona home on time, at 6:00 AM.

Once we were all in the van, I passed out sealed envelopes to every-one, keeping the last for myself. Each envelope contained one additional clue. They were to be opened as needed, starting with the youngest member of the family and progressing to the oldest.

Capri opened the first clue, which read, "Are you Happy about leaving the Valley". So, we headed to Happy Valley Road and opened the next clue. It read, "I 42, but I wish I-17." Next, we drove over to Interstate 17, where we opened the next clue. It read, "Let's cool off in Flagstaff." As we drove north to Flagstaff, speculations about Lake Powell and houseboats started to circulate in the van. I confirmed nothing.

At Flagstaff, the next clue read, "Put a new Page in the journal." So, we headed toward the town of Page, Arizona. At this point, the kids began dreaming of fishing, water skiing and boating on beautiful Lake Powell. Some, however, were still hoping that we were actually headed for Zion National Park, Bryce Canyon, or the North Rim of Grand Canyon.

As we crossed the Navajo Reservation, we passed many stands where the Native Americans sell their jewelry. At one of them, I pulled over, telling the family that I had heard a funny noise coming from the trailer. I jumped out, walked around the van and opened the sliding door. I then asked for the next clue to be read. It said, "I never learned to play the Tuba." We all looked around and spotted a sign that said Tuba City, directing motorists to the highway on the right. In no time, we were on the road again and headed for Tuba City. Once there, then next clue was read: "Have you ever stood in four states at one time?" Immediately, we headed to Four Corners, where the clue read, "The last time we were in this town, some nice man bought our entire family ice cream sundaes." Everyone remembered this event, and they remembered that it occurred in Durango, Colorado. So, off to Durango we went. When we arrived, yet another clue was read. This one instructed us to head northeast. We drove for about 30 miles and then arrived at the Five Branches Campground at Lake Vallecito.

As we pulled into the campground, I opened and read the last clue, which told of all of the activities for the week. It included camping on the shore for the week, one day's rental of a fishing boat, a dinner cruise on Wednesday for Joyce and me, hiking, fishing, swimming (for the hearty), a ride on a houseboat at night, naps and relaxing in the pines. All were excited, and the week turned out as much fun as all of the anticipation.

You Have Six Teenagers?!

Since the first six of our children were born rather close together, it was inevitable that one day we would be blessed with six teenagers at the same time. We have never thought of a young person as being a problem child. Far too often, kids are condemned by their parents way before they reach those special years in which their bodies and their minds take on exponential growth and development.

We actually looked forward to the teenage years. It is during this time that parents get to show the world what they are made of. If you think that a child kept you up at night during the first six months of life, just wait. I hope that every parent will give a teen the chance to express whatever he or she wants to talk about, whenever they feel like talking.

It is probably true that most who wander off down the wrong path do so while in their teenage years. Perhaps this is because from the time they are very little, they hear many people, including their own parents, say that they expect them to get into trouble once they become a teenager. Sometimes this is said lightheartedly, but it is said, all the same.

We love our teenagers! We let them know that. Their friends are our friends and we love them and let them know that. Who cares if they got the floor muddy when they walked in? The floor can be cleaned, but the opportunity to be close to your kids and their friends vanishes in a fleeting moment, and you don't want to miss that.

One day, as Blake headed out the door to go to school, Joyce told him that she would be making bread that morning. She told him that he could bring some friends home for lunch if he wanted to. At about 11:15 AM, fifteen high school students invaded our home and devoured four loaves of whole wheat bread.

Apparently, as Blake was leaving school with some of his friends, they told others. One of them yelled to some others that Blake's mom had made homemade bread for lunch. Soon, there was a caravan heading for our home. Blake didn't even know all the boys, but they were so gracious in their expressions of approval of the product that they were welcome.

So, during the time leading up to becoming a teenager, let your children know that the years ahead will be wonderful, and that you are looking forward to them.

You Have Six College Students?!

When you have six teenagers, they wind up going to college, eventually, and there was a time when we had six of them in college all at once. Three of them were married. They were all working part time jobs, living on campus, paying their own way, and getting the absolute most out of their college education. There was probably more learning going on outside the classroom than inside it.

Blake was a freshman in college and wanted to go to the university's Homecoming Dance with the limited resources that he had. Carmin helped him by preparing a beautiful corsage he could present to his date. Blake repaid her by referring other customers to her for their own corsages.

Since Trevor majored in Computer Science, he had the opportunity to become the neighborhood computer guru. In this capacity, he helped many other college students find or fix computers. In turn, he never hesitated to ask them for rides, since he didn't have a car.

When Monica was close to graduation, she wanted to student teach overseas, anywhere in the South Pacific. We had lived in Hawaii for a summer and she learned to love the Polynesian people. She came up with a plan where she could student teach during the summer if she could accomplish two major goals: complete 19 credit hours during the upcoming winter semester and raise all of the money for the trip during that same semester. Either goal alone would have been overwhelming. Still, she took the classes and worked three jobs. All of her hard work paid off when she got on the plane and headed for Samoa. She had a delightful experience that summer, and when she came back and graduated, she still had money in the bank. But more importantly, she had set a goal and had accomplished it.

Yes, when someone asks if we really had six kids in college at once, it sure is hard to keep the buttons on my shirt from popping off.

Dream Vacations Don't Have To Be Nightmares

In our home, we have made family vacations very special. Vacations are much needed breaks from work and routine, and they need to include as many family members as possible. They also need to be fun. They can be great tools in teaching families all about life. If you travel in close quarters with others for any distance, you will soon have many opportunities to practice good principles, such as "Love your neighbor." We put a lot of effort into making each trip, whether great or small, rewarding and full of long lasting and beautiful memories.

We always plan our vacations in detail. The entire family gets involved in picking where we go, what we will do, and how long we will stay. Needless to say, however, all requests cannot be granted.

The trip preparation centers around our "Vacation Notebook" (see Appendix A). This is a 3-ring binder that travels with us on each trip. In order to keep the kids happy while we travel, we have come up with some fun things to do along the way. We don't buy any souvenirs for the kids while on our trips. However, they can each earn money as we travel, and then they can buy their own. We have ten kids, and it could be a nightmare for us to keep track of all of the transactions on a long trip. We believe in training children in all aspects of life. So, we appoint one of them to be the accountant. This person makes a page for each child in our Vacation Notebook. On their page, a record is kept of the child's money earned and spent. Since we believe in tithing (see glossary), a column for tithing is listed as well.

As a child earns money on the trip, he or she is given proper credit. As money is spent, the amount is deducted from their running total. We pay each child in cash for the amount of money, if any, that they have earned, but not spent, while on the trip. If they wish, each child can also give us money and get a credit posted on their ledger before the trip. This means that when we go into a souvenir store, we don't have ten kids running around with their wallets out trying to buy things. Joyce or I pay the bill, and as we drive away, the accountant will make all of the entries in the book. A child is not permitted to spend more money than he or she has on the books for the trip, and they are not allowed to borrow money from anyone. They know that if they want to buy something, they must earn the money first, pay tithing, and then they can buy it. This is how life works, so this is a great teaching tool.

Over the years, we have come up with some fun ways for the kids to earn money as we travel. Years ago, we started the I-Spy game (see Appendix A). This consists of a list of over 50 animal and scenery sightings, each with a set value. Each day of the trip, the first observant child to spot something on the list earns the corresponding amount of money. A child can only get credit for a given sighting once. The next day, someone else can make money from spotting the same thing. When they see something, they are to say "I-Spy," and someone over eight years old must confirm the sighting. We keep some color picture books in the car that show birds, mammals and reptiles to help us identify what we see. It is not uncommon for an alert child to earn a couple of dollars in one day as we drive through the Rockies. One time, as we drove Interstate 19 from Tucson to Mexico and back, we added a new twist. The kids had to say "I-Spy" in Spanish: "Yo Veo." More than the reward earned, the I-Spy game has proven to be invaluable in keeping the children alert to their surroundings as we travel. They rarely ever ask, "Are we there yet?"

Another time, we established a goal for everyone to learn Morse Code by the end of the trip. If someone could signal and receive the characters of Morse Code, they would get a reward. Anyone who could successfully signal and receive a ten-word sentence from a Hardy Boys book would get another reward. By the time we arrived back home that year, all of the children knew Morse Code.

We also read books out loud while we travel. This is a great way to keep everyone occupied and interested. Sometimes it's a good mystery, like the Hardy Boys or Nancy Drew. Other times it's a book about our destination.

In Yellowstone, Joyce and I set up a family compass course with red licorice buried under some leaves. We divided the kids into two teams and had fun watching them try out their navigation skills. When one group determined that the prize must be in the middle of Yellowstone Lake, I took the opportunity to show them their mistake. They started over and worked at it until they got it right. They learned!

In Seattle, we took a half day boat cruise that taught all of us how canals and locks work. At the time, Capri was seven, and after our vacation that year, she had fun explaining how they worked to anyone who would listen.

Just prior to a trip to Cincinnati, which is where I grew up, I made up a 100 Question Quiz about my youth and the area in which I lived. We gave it to the kids before the trip, and they knew very few answers at the start. On the trip, however, we made it a point to *show* them the answers to all the questions. By doing so, they became more familiar with their dad's background, and they learned it in a fun way.

On another trip one year, we headed to the historical sights of the Eastern US. We knew that we would be visiting Gettysburg along the way. So, as we traveled, we read some books to the kids that told about this great place and what it meant to our nation. We told them of the famous address that President Lincoln had given there, and then we challenged them to memorize it. They answered the challenge and we stood as a family and recited the Gettysburg Address, verbatim, on the same spot where President Lincoln stood and uttered those same words so long ago.

Vacations with your family can be wonderful adventures, and they can also be excellent learning experiences for everyone. All you have to do is a little planning and preparation ahead of time.

Photo # 2: We stood as a family and recited the Gettysburg Address on the same spot where President Lincoln had first uttered it more than 120 years earlier.

Treasure Your Family Mealtime

Mealtime in the home can be used to promote family unity. Reserve the morning or evening meal for pleasant conversation, good stories and compliments. Make mealtime sought after by family members so they look forward to filling their hearts and minds, as well as their stomachs. Compliment, encourage and praise your kids often. Use this time to informally educate them on a variety of subjects.

For many years, I have read biographies and histories of great people during lunch at work. I would come home and discuss these at dinner in order to enlighten family members about Lewis and Clark, John Wesley Powell, Conrad Hilton, Ross Perot, Sam Walton, Captain James

Cook, General Colin Powell and many others. We have had many great discussions about these history books. It has only taken a small effort on our part to make our mealtimes constructive, interactive and educational. And the rewards have been many.

Where Are the Dads?

School field trips are lots of fun, but where are the dads? I can't think of a better use of a vacation day (maybe only a half day) than to show your children how much you care by going on a field trip with them. I have been on many, including visits to a local museum, to a huge basketball arena, and to a farm. Each time I go on a field trip with one of the kids, I always hear a similar comment pass from one teacher to another. It goes something like, "Wow, a dad actually came on this field trip! How did you manage that one?"

One year, Carmin went on a field trip to Disneyland. She was in the high school choir, and the choir and band were performing at Disneyland that year. I got to go along as a chaperone. We had three buses filled with wonderful high school students, and it was a very busy eight-hour drive over to Anaheim, California from Phoenix. These kids were wired! There was virtually every kind of personality represented on each bus. Many of them were cheerful, friendly and happy. But then there was the kid who did not want to associate with anyone. There was the one who wanted to make sure that everyone knew that he was on the bus. There was the inquisitive kid who had to figure out how everything worked. There were those who were too good for everyone else and, of course, there were those who tested the authority of the leaders to see how much they could get away with.

The young man sitting next to me was playing rap music really loud on his handheld boom box. He seemed to notice that I didn't care for his choice of music, even though I didn't say anything about it. I just wanted to get to know him and become his friend.

As the trip progressed, it soon became dark, but never quiet. In fact, the darker it got, the louder everyone became, since they couldn't see those to whom they were speaking. Hours later, we were at the motel, and there's a whole other story about trying to keep boys out of the girls wing and vice versa. But suffice it to say that we did it.

The next day at Disneyland provided me with several opportunities to help some of the kids—since they needed someone to hold their cameras, sweatshirts, food, souvenirs and a multitude of other stuff while they performed or enjoyed the rides. I'm sure I must have looked like a walking closet. A few of the kids were hesitant to try some of the rides, but I was able to convince most to try them, and I went along for moral support and fun. They were becoming my friends.

After spending the first half of the day at Disneyland, we visited the beach until dinnertime. I had tons of fun showing the kids how to body surf. I warned them not to get too much sun, or they would regret it later. They may have heard me, but they didn't listen. Almost all of them got sunburned to some degree or another. Luckily for Carmin, she listened to her dad.

After leaving Newport Beach, we drove straight to a fast food restaurant, where it took a while to fill all of the orders for three busloads of teenagers. By now, their sunburns were really starting to get uncomfortable. I noticed a drugstore across the street, so I went over and purchased three large bottles of Aloe Vera. Before I even crossed the street and got back to the restaurant parking lot, the kids spotted me and started streaming out of the restaurant doors, heading toward me in anticipation of sunburn relief.

I spent the next hour distributing it to them, and then it was time to go. I put one bottle on each bus. All the way home, the kids were calling for Mr. Clifton to bring some more relief to their scorched skin. The guy I had sat next to on the trip down, who played the loud rap music, stood up and offered a public thanks to me for my green gel. He said that it would be a long trip home, and that everyone was sore and tired. So, he suggested that to repay me, no one should play any loud music. They all cheered and agreed. At last, I had a friend. This is one dad who is glad that he volunteered to go on a school field trip!

Camping In

During our two-year temporary stay in Naperville, Illinois, we were always trying to come up with creative ways to teach and entertain the kids. We have always loved to go on camping trips, but we didn't have any of our gear with us in Naperville. We really had no way to camp out, especially in the winter. So, we thought of a fun alternative, and we called it "Camping In."

We picked a wintry Friday night and set some rules. We turned off every light in the house and acted as if we had no electricity. We even turned the furnace down. We divided into two teams. The boys and I were on one team, and Joyce and the girls were on the other. The boys' team got the upstairs; the girls' team got the main floor. Nobody could visit the other's territory for the entire evening and night.

The boys and I took food upstairs and had our dinner on the floor. We sat around a fake campfire and swapped stories until we were all so tired that we fell asleep. The girls' team enjoyed a similar "roughing it" meal. They had the fireplace on their floor, so they got to sit around a warm fire and paint their nails, fix their hair, rub each other's feet and shoulders, and do girl things. Each team had no communication with the other.

This was a good way for Joyce and me to get a little closer to some of our kids. It was not real comfortable sleeping on the floor in a house with little heat (a house that had an empty king size bed close at hand), but our kids still cherish the memories of that evening of "Camping In."

Family Camping

By now, it should be evident that we are a camping family. We have camped all over the western US. Not only does it save money, it provides built-in entertainment. Each of our kids has learned a lot about the outdoors during these outings.

When we get to a campground, we have the girls race the boys to see who can get their tent up first. We have had compass course competitions, nature hikes, and many other educational activities that have taught all of the kids some valuable life skills.

One thing Joyce likes about camping is that we plan all of the meals ahead of time, and everyone shares the cooking duties. We have some Dutch Ovens that allow us to prepare a variety of meals. This system has provided a way for everyone to get involved each time we prepare food.

We usually attend the Ranger Program at the campgrounds we stay at, and we have always enjoyed them. One time, Trent and I took the three youngest girls to the bottom of the Grand Canyon, which is a nine-mile hike in each direction. When we arrived at the bottom, they learned from the ranger that when you take a break while hiking, it is best if you elevate your feet. I had known this and had been doing it each time we took a break on the way down. I had not explained to the kids what I was doing, or why. However, on the way back, everyone's feet were in the air each time we took a short rest break.

Photo # 3: On our camping trips the girls raced the boys who raced Mom and Dad in setting up their tents. Even our younger children learned to set up camp.

Fathers or Sons Outings

We have succeeded in passing on our love of camping to each of our kids. The boys, in particular, are all avid outdoorsmen. We have had some wonderful experiences over the years. Every year, we get to go on a special campout that is only for men and boys. It is referred to as the Fathers and Sons Outing. I prefer to call it the Fathers *or* Sons Outing, since men can come along even if they don't have any sons.

Ever since Trevor was old enough to go, I have taken my sons and joined up with 50 to 100 other men and boys for this one night campout. There is something special about being outdoors that can result in a bonding experience. I have made it a high priority to be there each year. Even when I am out of town, I have flown back just for the event. It has provided some great memories that we will cherish for a lifetime.

Photo # 4: Clifton men on a Fathers or Sons Campout.

Why is Dad Whooping Up On Blake?

When we lived in Arizona, we were invaded with scorpions. They were everywhere, and several of us got stung. We learned about their habits and tried to protect ourselves from them best we could, but sometimes we just couldn't help but encounter them. We weren't the only ones who had this scorpion problem. Many of our neighbors did also.

On those long, hot Arizona summer nights, it was often more comfortable to sleep out on the trampoline than inside the house. We had a trampoline that was in our sand play area, and it was a perfect place to spend the night. The kids loved it. On any given night, several of our kids would be out there. Joyce and I spent many evenings on that trampoline telling stories to the kids and talking about constellations as we all watched the skies for falling stars.

One night, as the kids headed out to the trampoline with their pillows and blankets, I heard Blake yell. I ran out to see what the problem was and he told me that he had just been stung on the backside by a scorpion. He said that it was still in his shorts and he wanted me to slap him back there to kill it. It was the first time in all of my parenting experience that one of my kids had actually asked for a paddling! I obliged. Soon, the other kids, who were still in the house, gathered at the window and asked why I was whooping up on Blake in the sand pile. It must have been quite a sight, but we got the little fellow and he will never sting again!

Dacia Gap

In preparation for the 2002 Winter Olympics, Salt Lake City and the surrounding area made major modifications to the Interstate Freeway System. This went on for several years prior to the Olympics event. The local residents got used to the detours, closed roads, and traffic jams. This also changed the skyline of Salt Lake City forever as brand new overpasses, bridges and walls were constructed where there were none before.

As we were driving through town one day, we saw an overpass being built. It was completed on both ends, but had not yet been joined in the middle. As we drove, I pointed this out to the kids and told them that a certain man had invented a good way to save money on freeway expenses. His plan was to build both ends of an overpass, and when they got within 100 feet of each other, they would stop construction and install ramps going both directions. The cars would drive along, hit the ramp and then fly through the air to reach the other side. I told them that not only did this save money on construction costs, but it also kept pedestrians and bicycles off the freeway. I also told them that this would reduce the effort for the snowplow, since there was about 100 feet less of freeway for them to plow. I went on and on with my elaborate story, telling them that the man had won an award for his idea, and that we were currently looking at an overpass built according this man's plan.

All of the kids were asleep during my oratory except Dacia—and she believed every word I said. I told her to wake the others and explain it to them. She did so, and they immediately began to challenge her. Finally, Dacia saw me smiling and realized that I had been kidding. From that moment on, we named that stage of an overpass construction "Dacia Gap." We have since seen them in other places over the years, and we always point them out to Dacia. She laughs the loudest of anyone each time.

Hi-Yo Silver

We moved into our new home in Utah in the middle of May. Two weeks later, on Memorial Day weekend, I had a list of "to dos" a mile long. We had begun to wire the entire house ourselves, but the job wasn't finished, so that was the first thing on my list.

That Friday, I left work at noon and headed home. When I arrived, the concrete men were there. I asked them to wait until I laid some black ABS pipe in the sidewalk forms before they poured the cement. That way, I could later add wiring or plumbing if needed. They agreed and I got to work. Unfortunately, we didn't have enough pipe to finish the job, so Joyce volunteered to go to town and get more. She suggested that I take a break and go horseback riding with Monica while she was gone. That sounded like a great idea to me, and Monica thought so as well.

I got on our white horse named Silver and Monica mounted Cheyene. We rode to the reservoir under cloudy skies. The temperature was about 55 degrees, and it was a beautiful day. After riding around the reservoir for a few minutes, we started to gallop the horses. As we rode along the mountain, our right side was toward the uphill grade and our left side was toward the downhill slope.

Monica was ahead, and apparently, Silver didn't like that a bit. Suddenly, he started to buck. He lurched, and I was instantly thrown forward. All I could see was the ground coming up fast. I hung on desperately while he repeated this three more times in quick succession. He wanted me off his back.

I didn't want to dismount headfirst over the front of him, so I decided that I had better get off by myself, and soon. By this time, I had passed Monica, and as soon as I cleared her and Cheyene, I jumped off the left side of Silver and tried to land on my feet. Unfortunately, I miscalculated the distance to the ground, since I was dismounting on the downhill side of the horse. When my body finally connected with the ground, instead of landing on my feet, I landed on my backside—really hard.

Immediately, I tried to get up, but the pain in my back was so great that I started to black out. I then lay very still, knowing that any movement might make my injury worse. When Silver bucked me off, Cheyene decided to lighten her load as well. Soon, Monica was on the ground too, and both horses were galloping away. Luckily, Monica wasn't hurt.

I called out to her as she was picking herself up off the ground. I told her to go back to the house and call for an ambulance, that I had broken my back. She had seen my terrible dismount and knew it was a bad fall. Since she had been trained as a lifeguard, she knew to check to make sure I was well enough to leave alone. When she saw that I was stable, she quickly ran about a mile back to the house.

While she was gone, I laid there thinking about all the plans we had made for the summer, and all the work we had to do on the house. Now, things would be different. I always try to find something good in everything that happens in life. So, as I laid there on the mountainside, I kept telling myself that there must be something good that would come out of my unfortunate accident. Soon, I started counting my blessings that I had not broken my neck. After all, I was still alive.

After a few minutes, it started to rain. I had given some seminars on wilderness survival, and in particular, on hypothermia, so I was aware of the potential problem the rain would cause. I was now getting very cold. To make matters worse, it began to hail.

I tried to roll over, but almost passed out from the pain, so I just laid there on my back with the rain and hail pelting my face. Then, I noticed that my cowboy hat was lying within reach. Slowly, I reached for it, curled my fingers around the brim, and drug it toward me. Then, I placed it over my face.

After a long wait, I heard a voice asking me if I was all right. It was Blake. He was at home when Monica arrived and he immediately sprinted out to where I was. We shared a special moment as I relieved his concerns.

It seemed like forever before we finally heard the sirens approach. It took the paramedics quite a while to get to me because they had to cut some fences to get the ambulance close to where I was lying. By the time they got to me, I was already in the first stage of hypothermia, and I knew it. They tried to put an I.V. into my arm, but my veins were too small because I was so cold.

Finally, they got me into the ambulance. Joyce was riding up front as we made our way back through the field. The paramedics began cutting my clothes off, starting with my down vest. Soon, the fans circulating the air in the back of the ambulance began to distribute millions of down feathers. They were floating everywhere! When we finally arrived at the hospital, they warmed me up with heat packs and managed to insert an I.V. I was in the hospital for a week and off work for a month. Life changed for me that day, but I have mostly recovered now. I became even closer to two of my children that day: Monica and Blake. It was a traumatic experience, but it had its silver lining. By the way, we kept the horses for a couple of more years.

Chapter 2—Learning

Good parenting is based on providing a lifetime of learning experiences for the next generation. Life is an ongoing learning process. And often, we learn best by experience. In raising our children, we have always tried to learn something from all that we do and all that happens to us. We learn from others, and then teach our kids. We learn from our kids, and then teach others. First learn, and then teach.

Recitals

Many parents have a similar complaint: it's hard for them to get their children to practice their music lessons. Parents often invest substantial sums of money for music lessons, instruments, sheet music, and so on. Our home is no different.

One day, Joyce and I came up with an idea that worked pretty well. We told the kids that we would have regular recitals, right in our own home. I would be the banker and Joyce would be the judge. We told them that they would receive a small monetary award for every piece they played that Joyce judged as flawless. They could play as many pieces as they wanted, but they only got paid for the flawless ones. Once they received credit for a piece at a recital, they could not repeat it at a future recital. This proved to be a *good* incentive for them, but not a *great* one. Then, we came up with something more.

We typed up a long list of fun things to do, cut them up, and put them in a bowl. At the end of each recital, each child who had succeeded in playing at least one piece successfully would get to draw one prize from the bowl. We tried to be very creative in selecting these fun prizes. Most of the items didn't cost any money; they cost time instead.

We had a rule that if a child drew out a slip that they had already previously drawn, they must put it back and draw again. No money was paid, and no prizes were awarded until they were posted in their Book of Remembrance (see glossary). Among other things, the prize list contained the following:

Blank–no prize this time
Dad does your weekly chore once
Mom does your weekly chore once
Dad does your part of dishes duty for one week
Mom does your share of dishes duty for one week
Double pay
1 free "unmade bed" ticket
30-minute extended curfew for one night
1 free 3-minute phone call to a cousin
1 free video rental
1 free underage-driving lesson (on private property)
1 free frozen yogurt treat
Dad makes your bed once
Mom makes your bed once
1 new pillow
1 free frozen yogurt with Dad
1 free frozen yogurt with Mom

We found that the more creative we got, the better the results. We did allow them to swap prizes with each other, and that paid off when one of the kids over 16 got to trade their "1 free underage-driving lesson" for a "30-minute extended curfew" prize with a younger sibling.

The real treat for us, however, was in the bonding experiences we had when Joyce or I would do one of the kids' chores for them, or take them driving in the back yard, or take them out for a frozen yogurt. These small moments produced cherished memories that are just as important to us as the musical skills the children mastered.

Photo # 5: Dacia (age 10) gets an underage driving lesson in the back yard.

Traveling Animals

One fun thing that we do whenever we go on long vacations is to have each family member pick an animal they want to be during the trip. We pick animals that are native to the places we will be visiting, and it has been a great aide in teaching the kids about animals that they otherwise would not know anything about.

When we went to Yellowstone on one of our trips, Shayla, who was two years old at the time, was a Blue Heron. Before and during the trip, we studied about Blue Herons. We learned what they ate, where they nested, and how they cared for their young. During the trip, whenever we saw a Blue Heron, we would say, "There's Shayla!" She would get so excited. By the time the trip was over, Shayla knew as much as any of us about the Blue Heron.

One time, we took a trip to Alaska. Everyone picked out his or her animal. I had been a grizzly bear on a previous trip to Yellowstone a few years earlier, partly because I let my beard grow out for three weeks prior to that trip—so I thought the animal selection was quite appropriate. On this trip, the kids wanted me to be a polar bear because my beard was not as dark as it used to be. Shayla and I looked through a book filled with animals that live in Alaska and she picked out a puffin, which is a small duck-like bird that lives on the surface of the sea. It has a beautiful multicolored bill and dives for fish. The only time it comes to shore is to have its offspring. Everywhere we went in Alaska, Shayla pointed out every Puffin she saw, either in real life or in pictures of them. It added to the trip.

I will warn you that although this is a fun and educational game to play while traveling, it can have one negative consequence. For example, on one trip, when Blake was two and a half, he innocently suggested that his mom's animal should be a hippopotamus! After that trip, she became much more involved in picking her own animal.

Raising Chickens or Raising Kids?

One day, a friend of ours came to town and gave Trent a book all about a chicken tractor, which was really nothing more than a portable chicken coop. The idea was that you move the coop daily to give the chickens fresh ground to work over. They act much like a tractor in clearing out weeds and bugs, and they also fertilize the ground. The idea sounded like a good one, and Trent had always wanted to raise chickens, so we gave it a try.

We designed a steel frame on wheels, with chicken wire sides and a wooden lid. I taught Trent how to weld, and we welded the frame. Inside, there were two compartments: an open area and an enclosed area with roosts for laying eggs. When we finished building our chicken tractor, we got some other equipment—such as a heater, a feeder, and a watering tank. Then, we ordered our chickens.

When the chickens arrived, we had to keep them at a neighbor's house for a while, since they were too young for our shelter. Finally, the day came for us to stock our chicken tractor with a couple dozen chicks. Trent had a great time.

The chicken tractor project cost us more than we expected, by far, but Trent worked really hard at it. He put in many hours on the project, and even invested some of his own money. The three younger girls got involved too by helping Trent in any way they could. They especially loved to gather the eggs.

One day, a passing neighbor commented that I sure had put a lot of money into raising chickens. I smiled and told her that I was not raising chickens; I was raising kids.

Teddy Who?

When Shayla was two, we took a family vacation that included a trip to Mt. Rushmore. On the way, we read a book about the historic location to the kids. We learned how Gutzon Borglum had designed and supervised the carving of the mountain, and how each of the four presidents was chosen. Washington represented the beginning of the nation, Jefferson represented the expansion of the nation, Lincoln represented the unifying of the nation, and Roosevelt represented the industrialization of the nation.

As we traveled, the kids learned many good facts. However, it was obvious that Shayla, being only two-years-old, didn't get much out of our discussions. So, we started working with her to teach her the names of the four presidents. The dialog went something like this:

> Sibling: "George…"
> Shayla: "Washington!"
> Sibling: "Thomas…"
> Shayla: "Jefferson!"
> Sibling: "Abraham…"
> Shayla: "Lincoln!
> Sibling: "Teddy…"
> Shayla: "Roosevelt!"

We all clapped each time she got the names right. When we finally arrived, we hurried to catch the evening program in the amphitheater. It was a very patriotic program where an actor portrayed each of the four presidents. The actor explained in detail why their faces were up on the mountain, and what they represented. The monument was not meant to honor the four presidents as much as it was meant to honor our nation and four important periods of its history. After the four actors spoke, the lights on the mountainside were lit in a very dramatic presentation. It was tearfully breathtaking.

After the program was over, we walked back to the parking lot with a large crowd of other tourists. Shayla was half asleep on her brother's shoulder. One of the kids started the name game we had played with Shayla in the car. It went something like this:

Sibling: "George…"
Shayla: "Washington."
Sibling: "Thomas…"
Shayla: "Jefferson."
Sibling: "Abraham…"
Shayla: "Lincoln."
Sibling: "Teddy…"
Shayla: "Bear."

Then, Shayla fell asleep as the crowd chuckled with a quiet laughter. That moment of humor and sweet innocence eased the tensions of those around us who were hurrying to get to their cars.

Simon (Always) Says

Years ago, we decided to play a Home Night (see glossary) game with our younger children called Simon Says. However, we adjusted the rules so that Simon "always" says. This proved to be very effective in teaching really young children the basics of obedience. We had the whole family participate so the younger ones could see that their older siblings knew how to obey too. The entire family sat on the floor and participated. We would alternate clapping (Simon Says: Pat a cake) with each command. The clapping was used to reinforce obedience. After all, what excites a young child more than to have everyone in the room clapping for them after they have done something right?

Here is an example of how the game goes:

Simon Says: Pat a cake.
(Everyone claps.)

Simon Says: Hit the floor.
(Everyone says "floor" as they continually hit the floor.)

Simon Says: Pat a cake.
(Everyone claps.)

Simon Says: Hands on head.
(Everyone says "head" as they put their hands on their head.)

Simon Says: Pat a cake.
(Everyone claps.)

Simon Says: Hands on knees.
(Everyone says "knees" as they put their hands on their knees.)

Simon Says: Pat a cake.
(Everyone claps.)

Simon says:…

Have You Read Your Book?

When I was in the seventh grade, I was in an advanced math class. I liked math and did well with it. However, it was my dad who taught me a math lesson that helped me throughout the rest of my school days—and in every class.

One day as I was sitting at the kitchen table doing my math homework, Dad happened to walk by. He saw that I had written the letter "M" hundreds of times on several sheets of paper, and he was curious to know what I was doing. I told him that my assignment called for me to write the number one million in Roman numerals. I told him that a million was one thousand times one thousand. I said that in Roman numerals, the letter "M" represented one thousand, so I was in the process of writing it a thousand times.

He shook his head and asked me if I had read my book. I told him that I had skimmed through it. He then asked me to let him see the book. After only a moment, he was pointing to a page in the book that explained that if you write a Roman numeral with a line over the top of it, it is the same thing as multiplying that number by a thousand. Then, he wrote one "M" on the page and put a line over the top to represent one million. It made me feel rather silly that I had not read the chapter in enough detail to learn that simple fact.

From then on, whenever I went to Dad with a homework question, his first question was always, "Have you read your book?" I have since passed this valuable question on to my own kids in a like manner.

Apartment Life

We have sent several kids off to college. Most of them have only traveled ten miles to campus. However, in each case, we have encouraged them to live on campus in a dorm or apartment. We feel that living on one's own is a big part of the college experience. It provides the young person with opportunities to get along with roommates, improve their cooking skills, and to learn all of the responsibilities of household management. In addition, it is better to learn to live with others before marriage so that when a spouse enters the picture, getting along is not as challenging.

Kids who leave home and go to college are no longer under the watchful eye of their parents. This means that they set and maintain their own curfews. They decide what TV shows and movies they will watch. They decide how late they will stay up.

In our case, we did not provide a car for our kids while they were at college. They learned to walk to get around, and they all knew where to catch the bus. They also learned how to respect the property and feelings of their roommates—and how to give, serve, share, tolerate and love. Living with roommates was half of their college education.

Books and Tools vs. Games and Toys

Years ago, we decided to give our children more books and tools as gifts for Christmas and birthdays instead of so many games and toys. The payoff has been overwhelming. When we had young sons, I made sure that they had tools that were their own. I even put colored tape around each tool so they would not get them mixed up with my tools. They were never to use a tool that did not have tape on it. In this way, I could limit their use of the more dangerous tools until they were ready for them. Today, our teenagers know how to install insulation, hang drywall, paint, cook, sew, fix various things and grow a garden. The boys also know how to fix bikes, cars, wire a house, frame a house, remodel a cabin, weld, and do many more home repairs. Each project they learned how to do left them with not only added skills, but also some great lasting memories.

We have a series of books called the "Value of..." that helps those learning to read improve their reading skills. We pay our kids money if they read. Anytime they want to earn some spending money, they can pick up a book and start reading.

For example, I have read the entire journal of Lewis and Clark from cover to cover (1300 pages), and once, Blake read all three volumes to earn some spending money. We have books on every war our country has ever been in, and several books on US presidents. We also have biographies of successful people that make great reading and a delightful way to earn some money.

Photo # 6: Trent and Blake working on their bicycles with their own tools.

Photo # 7: Kids hanging drywall in the basement.

Photo # 8: After I broke my back, Grandpa came to help two boys finish the basement.

Computers are Tools

All of our kids over eight years old know how to use a word processor to a different degree. In our home, the Eagle Scout project and all associated paperwork is typed into the computer and printed out on the printer. We own several PCs, and sometimes I have to stand in line to use one.

We have taught the kids how to use e-mail to effectively communicate with others, but we discourage the forwarding of e-mails. Quite often, a child may get a message from someone that might contain things he or she may not understand. Sometimes they can even contain inappropriate material. If they were to forward that on to dozens of friends and family members, they are, in essence, endorsing things they would never have written on their own. By only allowing original e-mails, we have eliminated this potential problem.

We do not allow our children to "chat" on the telephone, so it follows that we do not allow them to "chat" on the computer either. Many problems associated with the Internet have risen from unknown people becoming acquainted through "chatting." In our home, computers play a big part of the family income. To me, they are great tools if used in the right way. Today, it is easier than ever to misuse computers, so care must be used when exposing children to them. However, used properly, they can become a real advantage to a family.

Besides my software business, we use computers to write histories and journals, send letters to others, keep track of addresses of extended family members, trace our ancestors, practice math and other skills, communicate with grandparents in another state, and keep track of my out-of-town assignments. It is a great tool to teach children how to perform research. It is also great for banking, paying bills, and budgeting both time and money.

In the next generation, a computer may prove to be more valuable to a family than a car. Therefore, children need to be taught good things to do on a computer. Just as cars, phones, TVs, videos, and CDs can be used for good or bad—so can a computer. However, because of the global nature of it, coupled with its rapid growth and increasingly more affordable price, the computer has the potential to be much more destructive than any of these other modern conveniences. Regardless of this fact, with proper love and parenting, it can become a blessing to a family. If your kids don't learn to use a computer within the walls of your own home, are you prepared for them to learn it elsewhere?

Read While You Travel

As previously mentioned, we read to our children as we travel. This helps to pass the time and teaches them many things as well. Once, we pulled into a restaurant parking lot to grab dinner, but nobody wanted to eat until we finished the exciting chapter of the book we were reading.

In addition to numerous books related to our religion, we have books on historical sights around the country. We stop at historical markers along the way while traveling in order to further enlighten our knowledge of the area. We have traveled to many places and read many books about those areas. Later, when the children study these places in school, they have an advantage because they have been to these places and read about them. They find the material covered in school more interesting and enjoyable, and they are able to contribute to class discussions.

Passive Vs. Active Entertainment

In general, we have divided entertainment into two categories: passive and active. Passive entertainment is accomplished with little or no effort on the part of the receiver. It includes such things as watching TV or movies. Active entertainment includes such things as cooking, sewing, gardening, working, scouting, building something, bike riding, hiking, reading, learning, teaching, playing sports, and volunteering service. We have found that pursuits of entertainment along the active category produce a much better environment for raising children. It is very important that we, as parents, practice this preferred selection of entertainment as well.

The 100 Question Quiz

The year we planned a vacation to Alaska, we told the kids that we would take care of the motor home, the food, and the transportation costs. However, they would each be on their own as far as extra activities were concerned. Alaska offers many wonderful, wholesome activities that are inviting. They wanted to take a whitewater rafting trip, ride on a real dog sled, and go fishing in the Kenai River for salmon. These were to be paid for out of their modest budgets, so we cooked up a special deal for them. We do not hesitate to invest in the education of our family.

I bought some books on Alaska, and then made up a hundred-question quiz. We told the kids that if they each took the quiz, whatever percent they got correct on it would be the percent that we would pay toward their extra activities while on the trip. The quiz would be open book, and each child would have a total of 90 minutes, minus their own age, in which to complete the quiz. For instance, a 16 year old would have 74 minutes to complete the quiz.

The quiz consisted of facts about the "Land of the Midnight Sun." Before we ever left on our trip, the children had read the books and asked lots of questions, and then they had taken the quiz. The scores were all in the 90% range, and they all felt really good about their accomplishments. They were glad to know that we would pay that percentage toward their activities, and we were glad that they had learned so many facts about Alaska.

Our plan paid off nicely. While we toured the state, the kids recognized and recited many things they had learned—such as the names of the five kinds of salmon, the fact that Alaska was the 49th state, what made the northern lights, why it stays light all night in the summer and dark all day in the winter, and that Alaska had an earthquake that measured 9.2 on the Richter Scale on Good Friday of 1964 that caused a 40 foot tidal wave. They learned all about Denali, as well as Mt. McKinley, the highest peak in North America. They came to know all about the native Alaskan plants, animals and people. They also learned about tundra and taiga. We were thrilled for the learning experience and their desire to see what they had read about.

This plan worked so well that a couple of years later, when I took a temporary job in Louisiana, I made up another quiz on that state and on the Mississippi River. We gave it to all ten kids and the three married children's spouses. The scores averaged more than 86 percent, and it was fun for all.

One year, we made up a quiz on Yellowstone as we spent eight nights there. The format for this quiz was to have two teams. We put spouses on different teams. Each team member, in order, was to answer a question verbally. They were allowed to seek help by asking one lifeline question of another member of their team. However, each team member could only ask one lifeline question, and each team member could only answer one lifeline question. In addition, each team could research one question by spending sixty seconds looking in a book for the answer.

Monica had just returned hours before from a long flight, and she had not been able to study as much as the others. Her team had used all of the members for asking for help except for five year-old Shayla. The question was asked of Monica, and she did not know the answer. She had to rely on the support of her youngest sister to help her. Shayla came through with the correct answer, much to the delight of both teams (not to mention her proud parents).

Everyone is looking forward to the next quiz. Imagine that…thirteen young people who actually *want* to take a quiz! I love being a dad!

High School Lasts Four Years

We have taught the kids that a student in the 9th grade is really in high school, even though they may attend "Jr. High." The grades they are earning while in 9th grade count toward their admission into college. They can participate in high school sports teams, as well as in music, dance and theatrical events. The activities they are participating in can be used on applications for admission to college and for scholarships. They are allowed to take certain classes that are given at the high school. In many parts of the country, 9th graders actually attend a high school, not Jr. High. By teaching our children that 9th grade is actually their 1st year of high school, we have instilled in them the desire to work toward advanced training and an education beyond high school.

Observe What Surrounds You

One summer when we lived in Tucson, we tried to teach the kids as much as we could about the area. One thing that Tucson has more of than Phoenix does is an abundant supply of saguaro cacti. There are so many around Tucson that there are not one, but two Saguaro National Parks, one on each side of town. We had driven along Tangerine Road on the north side of Tucson a few times as we traveled to and from Phoenix. There are many beautiful Saguaros along that road. We pointed some of these out to the kids, but we did not really emphasize them in any way.

Later, when we visited the Saguaro National Park that was on the east side of Tucson, we heard that somewhere in the park there is a Saguaro with 32 arms on it. We wanted to see it, so we drove along the park's eight-mile driveway and I told the kids that I would pay $0.10 per arm to whoever saw the Saguaro with the most arms on it. They were all eyes.

Soon, one shouted out that they had found a cactus with 7 arms. Shortly, the figure was up to 10. Then, someone spotted one with 15 arms, then another with 16. By the time the evening was over, the winning cactus had 17 arms. On the way home, I told Joyce that I thought there were more cacti and bigger ones along Tangerine Road than there were in the park.

The next time I drove along Tangerine, Capri and Shayla were with me, and we stopped and counted 21 arms on one Saguaro. That was the new family record. The next time Joyce and the kids drove along the same road, they came home and excitedly reported that Shayla had spotted a Saguaro with at least 30 arms on it. It had so many that they couldn't count them all.

I kept this in mind, and later, when we were once more traveling down the same road, they showed me this prized Saguaro. We stopped on the side of the road and counted at least 34 arms on the monster cactus. Later, I visited the site again and walked up to the base of the Saguaro. I counted at least 55 arms and determined that it was at least 50 feet tall.

Shayla won the prize for spotting the Saguaro with the most arms.

Photo # 9: Chuck is standing next to the "Shayla Saguaro Cactus". It is over 50 feet tall and has at least 55 arms on it.

Mental Math

There are times when I like to challenge the kids to do some math problems in their heads. I have them speak out loud so I can see how their thought process works. If they get stuck, I explain how to attack the problem with the mental math shortcuts that my dad taught me. This quick but challenging habit has paid off for all of the children, as it has helped them learn many skills—including basic math principles, logical reasoning, and problem solving.

Dry Riverbeds

When we lived in Tucson, one of the things that I kept stressing to the kids was that it was not safe to camp or hike in a dry riverbed. The reason is that there could be a heavy rain in the mountains that would feed the dry riverbed—and without warning, it could quickly turn into a swiftly flowing river once again.

To emphasize this lesson, I would point out a seemingly harmless dry riverbed whenever we crossed one. I would say to Shayla, "Let's pitch our tents in that dry riverbed." She would immediately respond with, "No! It's not safe to be in a dry riverbed." I can honestly say that she had that concept down pat!

A week after we moved away from Tucson, there was a flash flood that trapped ten kids in a dry riverbed. Seven managed to make it out on their own; the other three had to be rescued. Thankfully, they all survived the incident.

In life, there are dry riverbeds everywhere, and we should not play with them—even if they look safe. This story has served to reinforce our children's understanding that there are unseen dangers in a multitude of real life situations.

Learn, Then Teach

While I was growing up, circumstances did not lend themselves to allow me to learn to work with shop tools. So, as an adult, I had a desire to purchase every tool in the local hardware store! However, I disciplined myself and made a simple rule: I would not buy a major tool until I had taken a class on how to use it.

Soon, I was signed up for an evening woodshop class held at a high school across town. It lasted one semester and met once a week. This provided me with some great training, and I even made some fun projects. After taking the class, I bought a radial arm saw. I wound up taking the class two more times just so I could gain all the knowledge and experience that I could get.

After finishing the course each time, I bought a few other woodworking tools—such as a drill press, router, sander, and nail gun. I have enjoyed making some things that we needed around the house. Probably the most noticeable and most used of these woodworking pieces is the solid oak Lazy Susan that sits on our round dining room table.

Next, I took a welding class—and then I bought a welder. I wound up taking that class several times too, and even though I am not a world-class welder, I can stick two pieces of steel together and make them hold!

When it came time for us to build our house, I wanted the family to work together to wire it ourselves, not only to save money, but also for the experience of working together on a major, common goal. This was to be our house, and I wanted us all to have a hand in building it.

I couldn't find a class that taught this particular skill—so I bought some books and read them. Then, with the help of some experienced electricians, we wired the house. Trevor was just old enough to help on parts of it. One of our favorite pictures is of Trevor with his tool bag on, screwdriver in hand, standing beneath a light switch. He had just finished installing the plastic cover on that switch, and it is evident in the picture that he was so excited for having accomplished his task. As the kids have become old enough, we have enjoyed watching them develop interests in learning to build and repair things.

Photo # 10: Trevor was an electrician at age 4.

Blake and Trent have both taken shop class in high school. When they each started the class, the teacher was impressed at how well both boys respected the tools and how much they already knew. They got to skip much of the preliminary work and move right into making projects. Luckily, their high school just happens to have one of the best woodshop programs in the state.

Blake took the class for two years, and during that time, he made a chest of drawers, a nine-drawer dresser, and a cedar chest—all out of oak. Trent is in his third year of shop class. During his first two years, he also made a chest of drawers and a nine-drawer dresser. On his dresser, he added a full-width mirror with hinged sides. He has also made a baby-changing table, a king size bed frame with headboard, and matching nightstands. Trent even took the time to make Blake a mirror frame for his own dresser.

We get to keep the pieces they've made in our home until they have their own homes. Then, they will take their handiwork with them. Amy keeps reminding them how lucky their wives are going to be some day. As I look back on the difference between their knowledge of shop tools and my own at their age, I am glad that I have taken the time to learn, and then teach.

Photo # 11: Trent working in woodshop.

Papa Bear Whitmore

My employer once sponsored a wilderness survival class for employees and their families. The cost was $25 per family, which included lunch. The first four-hour session was held on a Friday and the remaining eight hours of the course was the next day. We managed to take eight of our kids to the class—and it was a real treat (not to mention a real bargain)!

We were the first ones there that day. The course was given in an auditorium that held hundreds of people, and it was filled by the time the course started. Since we love the outdoors, we were glad for the opportunity to receive training in this important subject. We had also recently moved to Utah from Arizona, and the survival skills needed in the new state were as different as night and day.

Our instructor was Papa Bear Whitmore, a world famous educator on wilderness survival. He has been on search and rescue teams all over the US, and has written several books and articles on the topic. He taught us some amazing things about how to stay alive if you get caught in the cold.

We learned that nobody ever freezes to death, since hypothermia will cause his or her body to shut down long before it actually freezes. He also showed us how to start fires using the traditional match or lighter—and also by using flint and steel, by rubbing two sticks together, and by using a magnifying glass. He even got a snowball and lit it on fire! We were equally amazed when he lit a special lighter stick, held it under a stream of water, and it did not go out. We learned all about the importance of achieving warmth if you're stranded in the wilderness.

He also taught us about not leaving your vehicle if you break down during a winter storm. The kids were especially attentive when he taught us about carbon monoxide and how it can kill you if you leave your car running. He told the story about a couple who got caught in a blizzard. The driver got out to get a blanket from the trunk and never made it back to the car. He had drifted away in the whiteout conditions and was not able to see the car, even though it was so close to him. He told of many other sad experiences, impressing upon us that the events were sad because people lost their lives or were severely injured—but what made them worse was that if the people would have had proper survival training, it would have saved their lives.

I didn't want this class to end. We were learning so many good things that all applied directly to many of the activities we participated in as a family. I bought Papa Bear Whitmore's small backpack-sized book and took it home to read. Its pages soon became highlighted and underlined. I then rehearsed with the kids all that we had learned. I was happy to find that they had learned a lot from the course; this was especially true of our teenage boys.

We held a Family Council (see glossary) and collected all of the things that we needed to put into survival kits for our vehicles. We set new rules about riding horses, including that we would never go alone and that we would always have warm clothing with us. We also made up "fanny pack" survival kits that each of us could wear when we went camping. That Christmas, Joyce and I gave most of the kids their own wool blankets. Did you know that wool is the best material to keep you warm because it is the only material that will do so even when it is wet?

I called up Papa Bear and bought 16 more copies of his book. That summer, I taught a class at our family reunion and handed out copies of Papa Bear Whitmore's book. Since then, I have had several occasions to teach the subject to other adults and children.

Life on the Bayou

The old adage, "Life is what you make it" is so true. In my job, there are occasions when I must travel out-of-town for long periods of time.

Therefore, I must get an apartment in another state. Joyce and the kids usually join me for part of the time that I'm away, if not all of the time.

I once took a seven-month job in New Orleans, Louisiana. At that time, all I knew about New Orleans was the following: it was home to the Superdome, it was on the Mississippi River, a lot of alligators lived there and Mardi Gras was held there each year.

I arrived four weeks before my family did, and I got a one-bedroom apartment on a bayou. For those who don't know, a bayou is a slow moving stream. It is filled with wildlife and it is not safe to swim in because of the alligators. But the complex had a pool, so we would be able to cool off during the hot, muggy days.

Since Joyce and three girls would be there for more than two months, I laid out a plan for us to do something every weekend. We ended up having lots of fun. For our anniversary, I took Joyce to spend the night in the largest plantation in the south. It's called Nottoway Plantation and consists of 53,000 square feet. We loved touring the historic building and staying in one of the original bedrooms. Later, we brought the kids there and gave them a tour too.

We also toured a Creole plantation called Laura Plantation. It was entirely different from Nottoway. The Nottoway Plantation no longer had its slave quarters, and it only showed one side of plantation life: the rich side. The Laura Plantation, on the other hand, still had slave quarters, and we got some wonderful pictures of the girls standing in front of them. We gained a better appreciation for the slaves after seeing where 20 of them lived together in a room that was not as big as a modern day family room.

Each weekend we would tour a new highlight of the area. Once we took a tour of the swamp and saw many alligators, including one that was 16 feet long. We rode a paddle wheeler on the Mississippi, and the girls learned all about the boats and the river. Next, we toured the site of the Battle of New Orleans and visited Vicksburg National Battlefield. We spent many hours there and learned a great deal about the Civil

War. We put our car on a ferryboat so we could ride across the Mississippi and teach the girls how the ferry works.

We also visited a battleship that is now a museum in the Mississippi River. We learned that there are 300 billion gallons of water that flow past New Orleans every day as it makes its way down the Mississippi River. We even stopped along the road, got out, hiked down among the weeds and mosquitoes, and touched the water of the Mississippi River.

We saw ocean-going vessels that were 75 river miles up river from the Gulf of Mexico. We saw nutria, blue herons, egrets, sea turtles, Spanish moss and much more. The kids got to learn the difference between a swamp and a marsh. We saw Cypress trees growing and we learned all about their "knees" that stick up. We even drove across the longest bridge in the world as it crossed Lake Pontchartrain.

When we left New Orleans, we had filled the kids with so many facts about the area and so many good experiences that they didn't have time to learn about some of the more undesirable things about the city—such as all that goes on during Mardi Gras. And that is why I love the old adage that "Life is what you make it."

Chapter 3—Work

Work is a fundamental opportunity that we have in life. It comes in many different shapes and sizes. Anyone can and should learn to work. It can provide a great setting in which parents can teach their children the lessons of life. Almost everything you ever wanted to teach your kids could be taught centered around the concept of work.

Work is learned most effectively when parents are working side-by-side with their kids, and work is valuable, whether or not the worker is "paid" for their labor. There are times when we reward our kids with money or other things for the work they do. However, they are also responsible for doing certain jobs or chores around the house for which they do not expect compensation.

We have also developed special projects in which the entire family will benefit from the completion of the project. An example is when we worked together to help build our own home. We have also done a significant amount of work for others in the form of service, and this is my favorite kind of work to share with our children.

All of our kids know how to run their own businesses, to varying degrees. This chapter describes some of the businesses in which we have been involved over the years. It will also describe many of the "non-earning projects" that we have done as a family. We include them in this chapter because they also depend on everyone producing a certain amount of work.

Raise and Sell Tomatoes

Selling tomatoes has been a very profitable business for the kids. At the beginning of each season, Joyce and I ask who wants to be in that year's tomato project. They each respond with their wallets by putting in $10 to raise enough money to get things going. Then, they have the opportunity to work hard all summer. When harvest time arrives, they always reap great rewards of several times their initial investment. In doing so, they have learned many valuable skills, including how to work as a team. For more information on our family tomato project, see the story below titled "A Cooler with a Sign and a Shoebox."

Carving Brings Bucks

One summer, Trent had the opportunity to learn the craft of carving bears out of logs using a chainsaw. After carving them, he sands them, scorches them with a torch to add shading, and then varnishes them. The last step is to put in the marble eyes. He has started selling these pieces around the neighborhood, and can hardly make them fast enough to meet the demand.

When Trent started the venture, he took some money out of his savings account to buy two very nice chainsaws and some other equipment and supplies. He has kept his eye on every penny that he has spent and collected, and he is excited about his profits. The job allows him to work at his own pace, and he is not committed if something more important comes up, like a family vacation. In fact, we spent part of a family vacation in the woods with him gathering lodge pole pine logs.

Trent has also learned how to make lodge pole pine beds, which have turned out nicely. And he recently taught Trevor how to make them. Now, Trevor and Amy have a beautiful bed that they made themselves (with a little help from Trent).

Money Just Swaying In the Breeze

Years ago, in Arizona, our girls bought 40 baby palm trees for $1.99 each and planted them in the yard where we irrigated the lawn. The only upkeep was to trim the grass around them after mowing. We soon learned to dig the grass back from the base of each tree once a year, and then no periodic trimming was needed.

In three or four years after the trees were big enough, we advertised in the newspaper. The ad specified that the customer must dig up the tree of their choice themselves. We consistently sold them for $20.00 each, and we ended up selling almost all of them. That was a return of about ten times our initial investment over three or four years. Wall Street would love that kind of return on an investment—and our kids have learned how to do it!

Work + A Sweet Aroma = Money in Bank

Joyce and the kids have done very well at their small baking business. Baking is becoming a lost art, and there is a tremendous market out there for quality home baked goodies. They bake cinnamon rolls, white and whole-wheat dinner rolls, orange rolls, white and whole-wheat bread, and specialty treats like "bunny bread" at Easter time.

They have sign-up sheets at the local schools for the teachers and staff to place orders one week in advance of delivery. On each Thursday night, a couple of kids make the dough and put it in the fridge. At 5:00 a.m. the next morning, Joyce and a couple of kids would start rolling out dough to fill their orders. As the kids leave for school, Joyce tosses the loaves into the oven, then she delivers them to the school later that day. When the kids come home from school, she pays them from the profits.

They also sell their products to the neighbors and at boutiques. Many customers have told us how much they have appreciated us providing home baked goods to their families. This has provided a great deal of income to those children who want to work for it. It also has helped them develop a myriad of skills—from working in the kitchen to learning how to advertise and sell products. There are also bookkeeping and general business skills that are learned along the way. Most importantly, they have developed a special bond while working countless hours together in the kitchen.

U-Bake Homemade Frozen Fruit Pies

One year, Joyce and the girls started making frozen fruit pies to sell at boutiques. They made and sold hundreds of frozen pies. Because of their huge success, frozen fruit pies were quickly added to the list of foods Joyce and the kids' baking business has to offer.

They place each frozen pie in a plastic bag. Attached to the bag is a small piece of paper with baking instructions. The advantage to the customer is that they can stockpile homemade pies for baking and serving later.

There are many different tasks associated with making pies. Someone gets out the flour and other ingredients and makes the dough. Then it is formed into one-pound balls and frozen. At a later date, someone thaws the dough and rolls it out to fit a pie pan. After the homemade fruit filling is finished, it is placed on the bottom crust. Finally, a top layer of dough is attached. The pies are then stored in the freezer until they are ready to be delivered to a boutique. At that point, the kids who work as the salespeople load up coolers with dry ice and pies, and then head off to the boutique to sell their homemade specialties. Usually, they don't even get in the door of the boutique before customers begin asking for their favorite pie. This has been a very profitable item, and it has taught the kids a great deal.

Harvesting Corn in the Desert

On two different occasions, we have gone out to a desert farming community to pick corn. The kids made flyers and passed them around the neighborhood. Then, they got on the phone to take orders ahead of time. We did not collect any money until we delivered our product. Each customer was told the date and time of day that the corn would be at our home for pickup. Many of our friends love to blanch corn and then cut it off the cob and freeze it. They bought it in large quantities from us because we gave them the best price. One year, we picked 2,500 ears in one day. The next year, we picked 3,500 ears—also in a single day! All of the corn had been pre-sold.

Each day consisted of several of us getting up early enough to leave the house at 3:30 a.m. It took over an hour to drive to the farm where the public was allowed to pick corn for a small fee. We could pick all of the corn we wanted, and were back home by noon, if not before.

We parked the trailer full of corn in the garage and called all of the customers to tell them that their corn was available. We were usually finished distributing all of the corn to the customers within an hour or two—then all that was left to do was count the money and take a nap!

It was a hard day's work, but a rewarding one. We harvested more than corn on those trips. We all learned how to get along with each other, as well as how to be cheerful on a hot Arizona summer day in a desert cornfield. The kids learned what really hard work is! They also gained skills in communication (dealing with customers); accounting (paying, collecting, counting and dividing the money); time management (selling all of the corn before it lost its moisture); desert survival (learning to drink lots of water, wear sunscreen, apply Chapstick, and wear a hat); planning (forming a crew and assigning tasks); estimating expenses (paying for gas and such); and farming principles (learning to pick only the ripe ears).

Making Hair Bows

One year, the girls learned to make hair bows to sell at boutiques. They made a ton of them, and although they did not make as much money as they had hoped to from the venture, they did okay. And each girl learned how to make custom hair bows.

Throw Your Own Boutique

Joyce has displayed her crafts and baked goods in boutiques for many years. A few years ago, we decided to have our own boutique in our home. We moved out most of the furniture from the main rooms and invited over 30 crafters to join our show. We opened the doors to over 1,000 people over a three-day period. It was good to have that many people involved in our family project. Each of the kids sold things that they had made themselves. The younger boys even made soup and salsa dry mixes to sell that rewarded them well for their efforts. They all worked hard to make the event a success, and aside from the money they earned, the experience of working together was a good one.

Arranging Flowers

Some years ago, our college girls took classes on flower arranging. This has provided them with a skill that has become a great money-maker. They have worked their way through college, in part, by making and selling corsages for dances (high school and college), Valentine's Day bouquets, wedding bouquets and arrangements, and funeral arrangements. They have made a lot of money and saved the family money as well by furnishing arrangements when we have needed them.

Squirmy Wormy

Not all of our adventures in earning money have been profitable. The one that our older kids will never forget is the worm business we once started. We had just moved from one state to another, and none of the kids had a way to earn money. So, I started looking in the local newspaper for opportunities they may be interested in. I passed up all of the "get rich quick" schemes that were advertised…well, almost all of them.

One did catch my eye. It said that if we were to purchase one gallon of this high concentrate liquid for $18, we could make lots of money catching and selling earthworms. The company (or person) selling us this liquid product would, in turn, buy all of the worms we could catch. It sounded simple and somewhat safe, so we pursued it.

We met the salesman, bought a gallon of liquid for $18, and then bought a 55-gallon drum for $7. That was our total monetary investment, $25.

The kids (bless their hearts) were with me on this all the way. The trick was to find old lawns that had been established for at least 10 to 20 years. We would then fill the 55-gallon drum with water and a couple of caps full of the liquid. Then, when the drum was full, we would tip it over and (supposedly) watch the night crawlers jump out of the ground.

We found our first home with an old lawn where the owners would allow us to try this technique. We must have had at least six of our kids with us that day, each armed with buckets to collect the worms. As we tipped the first drum over, excitement was in the air, but the worms were still in the ground. They did not come up from the ground as the product was supposed to make them do. We only saw a couple of them surface. We caught them and we moved on to another area of the lawn, and then tried again. We got the same results. After many tries, we caught less than a dozen worms. We returned home.

The next day, I called the salesman and told him of our lack of success. He agreed to meet us the next night at my co-worker's house. We tried it again and got the same results. This man was so sure he could find worms that he canvassed the neighborhood, asking complete strangers if we could pour this chemical on their lawns and catch all the worms that came up. He finally found an older lady who let us try. We got only one or two worms, so we called it quits and laughed all the way home. To this day, the kids remind me of how *that* project didn't work. What can I say? We tried!

Returns on Investments

Out of all of the entrepreneurial ventures we've tried, most have resulted in an excellent return on the investment of our money and time. However, one cannot always measure in dollars the eternal values learned through all of the cooperation, love, sharing, hard work, faith, diligence, organization, honesty, humility and service that we have experienced in the course of these family projects.

Suds 'N Duds

In our home, our kids help with all chores, and we try to make them as fun as possible. At the age of ten, each child starts being completely responsible for his or her own laundry. This includes everything from washing and drying to folding and putting away all of their clothes. To a ten year old, using the washer is fun. They learn that if they don't wash it, it won't be clean when they want it. By the time they are out of high school eight years later, they have probably done their wash over 400 times, and the excitement has worn off. However, the next year at college, they are usually hundreds of loads of wash ahead of their roommates. They can provide a great service as they give valuable advice on what not to wash with what, why something might shrink, or the dangers of adding bleach to some fabrics.

Let Me Dig It

Part of my approach to life came via my parent's training. An example from my youth will show this. One time, my dad made some extra money from an investment. With that money, we bought a couple of new cars, invested some in an oil well, and bought a swimming pool. However, Dad issued one demand regarding the swimming pool: we had to build it ourselves.

Now, we had never built anything bigger than a birdhouse, and we had no idea how to go about building a huge swimming pool! So, he contracted a company that would guide us as we built our own in-ground, 16' by 32' pool that had a deep end of 7 ½ feet. Instead of concrete, it had steel walls and a vinyl liner.

Dad got a bid from someone to dig the hole and haul the dirt away for $100. I was a freshman in high school at the time, and I had big arms and a strong back (and a thick head). So, I told him that I would dig the pool for $35 and save the family some money. To my later joy, he hired the man for $100. I sat there on that summer day and watched the man use his backhoe to fill his dump truck 22 times and haul the dirt away. I was shocked at how much dirt came out of that hole. Boy, did I learn the value of estimating before opening my mouth.

We then got into the hole and graded it by hand. Next, we installed the steel walls and bolted them together. Then, we put a sand base down and raked it smooth, installed the vinyl liner, and filled it with water. The entire process took only ten days. It was a great family project in which all participated. Dad did hire me later to lay the 569 patio bricks around the edge of the pool, and I still remember what a huge job that was!

We had many fun times using that pool, and we appreciated it much more because we had built it. We saved over $1,000 by building it ourselves. However, I now see that my parents were not trying to save money; they were trying to raise a family.

My sister got to visit our old house nearly 35 years later, and the pool is still there. Not one brick is missing from around it. I am not sure how long the pool will last, but the memories and their impact on my life will last forever. Thanks, Dad and Mom, for your efforts in raising *my* generation.

A Clean Kitchen in Ten Minutes Flat

One day, Joyce went into the kitchen late at night and found that the dishes were still dirty and the kitchen had not been cleaned as she had instructed. We held a Family Council and presented the problem to the kids. We came up with a plan, and it was very successful.

For each dinner, six days a week, the kids were to do all of the dinner dishes within ten minutes after I stopped eating my last bite. This included clearing the table, loading and starting the dishwasher, sweeping the floor, clearing all of the counter tops, cleaning the sink, cleaning the stove and microwave, taking out the trash, and even turning out the kitchen lights on a sparkling clean kitchen. If all was done within ten minutes, we paid each of the workers a fixed amount of money. If they didn't make it, they received nothing.

There were times when they would finish their meal before I did, and they would jump up and start the dishes. They learned to cooperate and share the work. Nobody got paid if the team did not make it. Sometimes, when there were a lot of extra dishes, or if we had extra people for dinner, I would let them work for about 5 minutes, then I would walk over and take one more bite of something. This would bring shouts of joy as they reset the timer for 10 minutes!

It really lifted their spirits and it lightened the family wallet, but that was okay. This was one of the best deals in America. We marked on the calendar each night that they succeeded and paid them at the end of the month. In keeping with the spirit of the Sabbath Day (see glossary), Sundays were done for free, so Joyce and I even helped them. We sometimes took their pictures while they did their work, and we took their pictures getting paid. Most of all, we celebrated clean kitchens! The arrangement taught them all some great work ethics that will last a lifetime.

Making Dough, the Old Fashioned Way!

It is very important that children be taught correct financial principles early. One thing that our children have learned is that you shouldn't go in debt to buy consumer goods.

Early one morning during a Labor Day weekend, Dionne, who was 13 at the time, came to us and said that the shoes she had wanted to buy all summer were on sale at a discount shoe store. She added that the sale would end that day. We asked her how much they were, and she said $10. I asked her if she had any money, and she said, "No." I then asked her if she knew what to do, and she said, "Yes." Without any further discussion, she went to the phone and called the neighbors. She said something like, "Hello, this is Dionne Clifton. I am making homemade cinnamon and dinner rolls today, and I wondered if you would like to place an order."

She soon had enough orders. She got out the flour and went to work making enough dough to fill the orders. By late afternoon, she had made her deliveries and had her money. She held out some for tithing, and then hurried to the shoe store. She got there five minutes before they closed and bought her shoes. She never asked us for the money. She knew how to make her own "dough"!

Let's Reap What We Sow

In our home, we make good use of fruits and vegetables that grow abundantly in our gardens, vineyards and orchards. We have invested in canning equipment, and during the season, it becomes a big family project to put up food for the winter. I probably get more involved than most men in this very important effort because I think every family member should participate. And you can learn many great skills that will pay off later.

One day in January, Trevor came home from college and brought a couple of friends home with him. They immediately went to the basement food storage room to get some fruit that Trevor had helped us can the previous summer. He told his friends that he liked to shop in the "campus grocery store." That was a good analogy, since you reap what you sow—and who needs good, nutritious food at a low cost (or free) more than a college student? He had learned a great lesson in life, and he was teaching it to others.

Photo # 12: Blake, Tanya, Monica and Carmin help peel peaches before putting them in jars as they help with the canning chores.

Family Gardening, Everyone Gets Involved

At his own expense, Trent planted seeds indoors in late winter in anticipation of providing the plants for the family garden when spring arrived. He succeeded, and we paid him about what we would have paid at the store for the plants. He got to plan and budget all the supplies, as well as schedule the deadlines to be met so that the plants were ready at planting time. He did a great job. As a result, we now get about a million seed catalogs in the mail every winter.

We have given each child his or her own garden plants and let them nurture the plants all summer. They get to learn all about how they grow. They also learn about watering, feeding, weeding, pest control and harvesting. They get a firsthand lesson on where food comes from. Then, at harvest time, they get to help us as we bottle the fruits and vegetables for future use.

Work, the Breadth of Life

Good work habits can provide more rewards throughout life than one can measure. At one time, we had two horses. This brought the great opportunity of work for our children. We made an equestrian chore chart. The three teenagers who were at home at the time each had an assigned chore, and they traded chores every three months.

One job was to feed the horses every morning. Another was to feed them every evening. The other was a set of weekly chores. It included moving hay from the tarp-covered haystack to the small shed, securing the tarp so the wind wouldn't rip it to shreds, maintaining the water in the trough, and shoveling manure.

One day, the wind blew really hard. The tarp came off the haystack and the teenager in charge of the tarp was responsible to fix the problem. If the tarp were torn beyond repair, a new one would need to be purchased—by the one who was responsible for the chore. Kids need to be taught to consistently do quality work and to take full responsibility for faulty work.

A Tight End and a Sewing Machine

We have seven daughters and three sons, and each is skilled at cooking, cleaning, sewing, building, repairing and gardening. In the fall of 1993, our son Trevor just may have been the only tight end in the state of Arizona who would come home from high school football practice and sew up his own jersey after it was torn at practice. And on her prom night, Carmin told her date how she had mowed the lawn that day before getting ready for the evening's activities. Just ask Monica and Tanya about how they put asphalt emulsion (tar) on the outside of the basement walls of our new home to seal out water. Ask Monica how she ran all the phone wire as she roughed in the phone jacks when we built our new house. Or, ask Tanya about the intercom wires she ran from the main station to every room that was to have intercom. If it needs to be done, our kids can do it!

Work or Play?

Around our home, work and play are the key ingredients to happiness. In fact, we like them both so much that we mix them up—and the kids are not sure which we are doing!

For example, one fall day we held a mini-Olympics for our 12-year-old son, Trevor, and some of his cousins and neighborhood friends. There were several "events" rolled into one. Here's how it went:

The kids started at the patio, ran to the basketball court, shot five free throws, ran to the swing, swung back and forth five times, did five pushups, did five jumping jacks, did five sit-ups, served a volleyball over the net five times, spelled their names five times, counted to 100 by increments of their age, grabbed a five gallon bucket, ran to the back fence under the peach and apricot trees, filled the bucket with leaves, ran to the trash can, dumped the bucket of leaves in the trash, and ran back to the starting point!

The one with the best time won the best prize, but everyone got a prize of some kind because they cleaned up all my leaves. Now, were they working or playing? We don't know either, but it sure was fun, whatever it was. And the yard looked great!

Working Smard vs. Merely Working Hard

Years ago, someone advised me to make sure to teach my children to work "hard." This is great advice; however, we put a twist on this advice as we think that it is just as important to work smart as it is to work hard.

Imagine that a person comes up to you and asks you to plow a 40-acre field. You can do it in many different ways. You could get a modern tractor and be done in no time at all. You could get a mule and plow the old fashioned way. Or, you could even get a teaspoon and take the rest of your life to accomplish it. In these three examples, the one with the hardest work is not the wisest choice. In fact, the one with the second hardest amount of work would not be the wisest choice either. We all know that it would be best to get a tractor.

In raising our children, we have tried to teach them to work "smard." This is a word that I have coined to mean "smart and hard." The combination is very important. As we have taught the kids to work, we have tried to find ways to teach them to be more effective and efficient in all that they do.

In the field of computer science, we have a concept called "multi-programming" in which a computer is programmed to do several things at the same time. In reality, a computer cannot do more than one thing at any one point in time, just like a human cannot. However, computers and humans can both be programmed (taught) to accomplish many different tasks at the same time.

Below are some examples of how our family has accomplished more in a given amount of time by working "smard":

Laundry Day
Let's assume that you have one washer, one dryer, and a clothesline. There are certain items that take a long time to dry in the dryer, and this usually causes a backlog on washday. However, if you plan to put those items on the clothesline, you need to make sure to **not** wash those **first**. Why not first? Because if you washed them first and then hung them on the clothesline, when you wash the next load, the dryer will be sitting there empty and idle while the second load of wash is preparing clothes for the dryer. This is a waste of resources. Instead, first wash a load of clothes that will go into the dryer. Then, wash a load of clothes that can hang on the line while the first load of clothes is still in the dryer. Alternate as needed and you are working "smard."

Multi-tasking
Suppose that you needed or wanted to do several things one morning. You want to start the computer and log onto the Internet, a process that takes about five minutes. You also want to cook some blueberry muffins in the oven, and it takes about five minutes for the oven to preheat. You also need to shave, and that takes about five minutes. So, go turn on the computer, then turn on the oven, and then shave. While you are shaving, three things are being accomplished for you. This is working "smard."

The Outside Phone
In our home, we have a canning patio outside where, on those warm summer days, we are able to can many jars of fruit each year. Needless to say, we spend a lot of time on the canning patio. However, as in most busy homes, the phone will often ring and take someone away from his or her canning efforts. So, I installed a phone outside on the patio, and

now work can continue, even when the phone rings. This is working "smard."

Shopping The Right Way

If I asked you to go to the store and buy a 3/4" drill bit that will drill into masonry, you could work hard by driving to every store in town until you found it. However, you could work "smard" by first calling around to find out the closest store that carried it, thereby saving time and resources.

Follow the Shuttle Bus

When I go to the airport, I often need to park my car in the long-term parking lot. If the lot is full, there will usually be several cars racing around the lot (working hard), trying to find a parking spot quickly so they don't miss their planes. Instead of joining them, I have a secret. I simply follow the shuttle bus. Then, I follow someone who gets off. They will lead me to their car and the next available parking space. The other drivers may work harder, but I work "smarder," and it pays off.

Black Plastic Gardening

When we went out into the garden one year, we found that the weeds had taken over! We had all been extra busy that season, and none of us had done our weeding. It wasn't easy, but we removed all the weeds. While we were doing this, we were all thinking that there must be an alternative. We were determined to come up with a better way to garden without creating a nightmare of weeding projects.

The next year, we bought a roll of six mil black plastic and put it over the garden right after tilling it. Then, we got some rocks to hold the plastic down. We cut holes in the plastic the size of a dinner plate, and then planted our crops in the holes. We put tomato cages over the tomato plants, which also helped hold the plastic down. We then watered by sprinkling for an hour. This showed us where all the puddles would be. We sent our youngest kids out there barefooted with nails to poke holes where all the puddles were. Soon, all the water was gone off the plastic.

Early in the season, when it was cool, the black plastic warmed the soil and helped the plants take root. Later, the plants shaded the plastic, so heat was not a problem. The only weeds that we ever saw were around the plants, and they were few and far between.

We have since switched from sprinkle watering to drip watering, with the drip lines lying under the plastic. There are side benefits to this kind of garden. For one, we always had access to the plants. Also, we can work in the garden right after a rain, since we can walk right out on the plastic without getting muddy.

In Arizona, we had a summer garden and a winter garden. We would buy one new plastic covering in the fall. After the winter garden was over, we would pull up the plastic, till and fertilize the soil, and then lay the plastic back down for the summer garden. After the summer garden, the plastic was not any good, so we started over each year. Still, one sheet did serve for two seasons. The cost of the plastic was not that much money compared to the problems caused by weeds more than six feet tall!

When we moved to Utah, we also installed this kind of garden—but we added a new twist. We can now have only one garden season per year, due to the cold weather. So, we decided to make the garden 100 feet by 40 feet and put tall "berms" (large mounds of dirt) on the edges of it. Each fall, we buy new plastic and install it, and then fill it with water. When winter comes, we have a 4,000 square foot ice skating rink!

We have gone to the second hand store and bought all the ice skates we can find for almost nothing. In the winter, when friends come over, they can enjoy ice-skating too. So, in a way, we do have a two-season garden in Utah. One season we harvest vegetables; during the other season, we harvest fun times. Both produce great memories.

Photo # 13: Happy gardeners because we use black plastic.

Photo # 14: Happy ice skaters because we use black plastic.

Chapter 4—Finances

Money is an item that man has invented to be used in business dealings to ease the transaction process. Teaching children (as well as adults) the proper use of, and respect for, money has been a challenge throughout the ages.

The proper accumulation and disbursement of money are very important subjects to be taught to the next generation. In their lifetimes, financial matters will become a greater part of their existence than we have seen in past generations. This is due in part because of the fast paced global world in which we now live. As the world in general moves from the farm-based families of yesterday to the Internet kids of tomorrow, money becomes a more important medium than ever. Unfortunately, you just can't barter with your favorite airline to trade a bushel of wheat for an airline ticket over the Internet.

As previously mentioned, we decided to not give our kids an allowance. Instead, we have tried to find more creative ways in which they can earn money. In particular, we have tried to tie their earnings to their hard work and learning—as this is how it is in the real world. The proper understanding of finances at a young age is a prerequisite to surviving in the world of the future. Therefore, parents need to work at this, and be good financial role models themselves.

Checking Account

When one of our sons or daughters turns 16, many new avenues in life open up for them. They can drive, go on dates, and legally hold a job. So, we feel that this is a good time to get them a joint checking account—with Joyce and me as co-signers. We have them keep all of their spending money in this account. They write checks anytime they need to spend money. We teach them how to balance the account and have them live within their means. We pay any banking fees until they are 21, or unless they bounce a check. We teach them that bouncing a check is a form of dishonesty and should be avoided like the plague. We put an extra $25 in the account, but they don't spend that money. We have them write a check to themselves for $25 that never gets cashed. This allows the check register to look like there is always $25 less than there really is. That way, there will always be a buffer of $25 in the account. Two years later, when they leave home, they will have had a couple years of supervised money management under their belts. They seem to be better off because of it.

Paying for College

When people meet us and find out that we have ten children, their first comment is usually regarding the cost of paying for college. They mention the national statistics that say it costs $250,000 to pay for one child's college education. So, when they find out we have ten kids, they want to know if I have 2.5 million dollars socked away. They are shocked when I tell them how we do things.

We have told our kids from "Day One" that we would not be paying for their college education. We have always told them that we would do all we could to teach them how to work their way through college. Half of this knowledge is how to earn money. The other half is how to not waste money. Both are equally important.

Throughout our children's lives, we have provided ways in which we could help them save for college by matching the money that they put into their savings accounts. This was done in order to establish the good habit of saving money for a goal. And it works!

As you can tell from reading this text, we have spent a lifetime teaching our kids about everything. They have learned many ways in which they can earn money. With that knowledge, they can become creative and think of just as many more. They have also learned to share with others. That's just how it works in a family with ten kids. They have learned to do without things that they really didn't *need*. They have also learned how to save and not waste money. Each is frugal in his or her own way.

To date, four of our children have graduated from college, and each has paid his or her own way. Tanya, who is married and has a new baby, is still pursuing her degree. Blake paid for his freshman year before he left on his mission. The rest of them are in line to pay their own way as well.

Each of our children knows that you do not need a fancy car while away at college. Most of them did not have a car until they got married or graduated from college. And then, they got whatever kind of car they could pay cash for. That means that our single kids walked all over campus. It was good for them.

They learned how to have a social life that was not money-centric. They learned to share an apartment with roommates to keep the cost of rent down. They learned how to fix economic foods and rarely ate out at fast food restaurants. They bought used books when they could and sold them back when the class was over. They even taught their roommates some of these skills that helped them save money too.

We have always thought of a college education as more than a way to learn how to spend the family's money. Our kids have learned how to wisely spend their own hard-earned money—and it has paid off.

Ultimate Thriftiness

If the shampoo bottle is full, people tend to use more than they do when it is almost empty. In fact, studies conducted in my own shower have shown that the first 50% of the shampoo is used up in the first 33% of the time, and the last 50% of the shampoo is used up in the last

67% of the time. Always keep the shampoo bottle less than half full so shampoo users will be more frugal in their use of it.

This theory can also be applied to such things as salad dressings, bottles of bleach, detergent, dishwasher soap, and other liquids. It's amazing to see how wasteful people can become in times of plenty, and how conservative they can be when times are lean. Real success just might be tied to those who can be conservative, even when times are good.

Financial Wisdom

We have taught our kids the following ways in which money and time can be invested to provide great returns:

1. Get a good education and maintain ongoing training.

2. Live within your means; don't spend more than you make.

3. Save a penny and it's worth two pennies earned, after taxes (see Appendix B).

4. Avoid unnecessary debt.

5. Have a savings account.

6. Have adequate medical, life, auto, home or renter's, and disability insurance coverage.

7. Have a clear will that describes your wishes; make sure others know where it is kept.

8. Be honest in your dealings with your fellow man, even the taxman.

9. If you want to buy something for $X, then first sell something for $X.

10. Maintain a year's supply; buy things on sale and save big time.

11. Grow as much food as possible; learn to eat what you grow.

12. Get the best job you can and invest in the education of your own children; more education should happen in the home than in the classroom.

13. Shop around.

14. Don't buy on impulse; plan your purchases.

15. Take a shopping list to the grocery store and only purchase items on the list.

16. Accept hand-me-downs; don't be too proud to wear them.

17. Put money *into* the spare change jar; don't take it out.

18. Have everyone take a brown bag lunch to school or work.

Auto Expenses

An automobile is a huge resource for a family. In 2001, the US government allowed businesses to deduct 34 ½ cents for every mile driven on company business. This is no off-the-wall guess but rather an actual calculated value after a great deal of research. And it is good to teach family members about the cost of driving and maintaining a vehicle.

Kids need to know that not only is speeding dangerous, it also adds heavily to the family auto insurance bill. The family needs to practice conserving miles on the vehicle by combining errands. Good scheduling, planning and communication are essential here.

Teach them to leave for wherever they are going early enough to get there in time, safely, allowing for an unexpected delay. Sit down with them and calculate how far it is to a frequent destination. Then, at the posted speed limit, figure out how long the driving time would be under ideal circumstances. Add on a few minutes for bad weather, stop signs, stoplights, heavy traffic or car trouble. Let them see the big picture that they cannot get there in "just a minute." They will drive safer all their lives if you teach them this while they are young.

Temporary and Permanent Savings

Each of our children has had a savings account that is divided into two parts: Temporary and Permanent. The bank only sees it as one account per child, but we have sub-divided the accounts in our own record keeping.

Money can be put into Temporary Savings and pulled out as desired by the account owner. This helps to keep money from piling up in drawers, closets and pants pockets (and hence washing machines). It earns interest for the owner and it is harder to spend. This kind of account is similar to what most people have for their children.

The Permanent Savings account is for money that is earmarked for three special future purposes: mission, college and marriage. Any money put into Permanent Savings can only be pulled out for one of these three reasons. As parents, we match money put into Permanent Savings so the kids have a chance to save for their future. This doubling of their money has worked well to encourage all of them to put lots of money into their Permanent Savings. It has been a great tool to teach them the value of saving. It is touching when a seven-year-old son brings us money to double and put away until he is 19. As adults, do we have that foresight to save something away for use 12 years later?

This requires extra bookkeeping on our part, but it has taught the children a consistent discipline through the years. For example, after an evening of babysitting, a daughter will pay her tithing and then leave most of the rest of the money on my desk with a note explaining how much is to be put into "Temp" and how much is to be doubled and put into "Perm."

Sometimes in the middle of dinner, I will shout "Ouch!" When someone asks what's wrong, I tell them that it was the family wallet crying out because of all of the "Perm" savings and matching going on these days. The kids love to hit the family wallet hard, and it thrills us when they do.

We'll Pay One Half

There are certain summer programs and activities that are good for kids, and we strongly support them. Among these are scout camps, girls' camps, sports camps, and youth conferences. We wanted to be sure that our kids had the opportunity to attend the ones they wanted to. However, we thought that if we paid their way entirely, these programs might lose their value. So, we have always had a policy that if a child wanted to go to camp or a conference, they had to pay half and we would match it. This has worked very well, and they have always been able to attend.

Sew What You Rip

You may have heard the expression, "Reap what you sow." It's a good concept, and we have a similar expression in our home: "Sew what you rip." In a nutshell, this statement says to fix things that need repair. Doing so has several benefits:

1. It saves money if you repair something instead of buying a new one.
2. It gives you a chance to teach your kids *how* to fix things, which will help them throughout the rest of their lives.
3. It provides a sense of independence because if they can fix it, they don't need to rely on someone else to fix it for them, or to provide a new one.
4. It teaches them humility; whatever they've fixed may still show signs of once being broken, but it's still functional and of value.

These benefits of thriftiness, education, independence, and humility are all related in the stories from the *Little House on the Prairie* series that Joyce has read to our kids over and over. Out on the prairie, people probably didn't have a way to buy new things every time they broke, so they had to fix them. It's wonderful that so many things can be taught with such a simple principle.

Motels and Crock Pots

If we ate out every night while on vacation with our family, the cost would be outrageous. Therefore, since we usually stay at a campground, we have all learned to fix Dutch oven meals and cook over an open campfire. However, we have occasionally taken vacations and stayed in motels. Therefore, we had to come up with an inexpensive way to prepare nutritious meals.

Joyce started taking a family sized Crock-pot with us. She would cook meals ahead of time, freeze them, put them in the cooler when we were ready to leave, and then thaw and heat them in the Crock-pot as needed during our journey. Joyce has become quite creative in preparing any type of meal for us in a timely manner. This has not only saved us money, it has also provided us with more nutritious meals. And just think of all it teaches the next generation.

The Auction Business

One day, a friend showed me an advertisement about a seminar being held at a hotel across town. The cost was only $10, and it included lunch. I usually avoid these things, but the subject was about auctions, which I was interested in. So, I told my friend that I would go with him.

At the morning session, the seminar speakers provided many tips on where to find information about auctions and how auctions work. After enjoying a great lunch, we attended the afternoon session and learned the tricks of this trade. Then, as the seminar came to a close—we got the sales pitch.

The group presenting the seminar was selling a set of books, cassette tapes and reference materials that were at least two feet thick. If you bought these separately, they would cost $2,000, but we could buy them that day for a special low price. Soon, I had my wallet out and bought a set.

I went home and studied the materials in great detail. There were auctions of every kind, and an ambitious person could make a lot of money by buying things at auctions and selling them at garage sales, swap meets, or in the classifieds. We thought that with the built-in labor force we had, and varied interests of our individual family members, we should do well.

Our First Auction–County Surplus

The first venue we attended was a county surplus auction. Since most auctions only deal with cash, I went to the bank ahead of time and withdrew a set amount. The following Saturday morning, Blake (who was ten at the time) and I headed to the county offices.

We inspected everything they had on display and watched as others bid on things. It seemed that things were selling for pretty low prices. As we watched, we learned how to bid. Soon, I got pretty good at "reading" a bidder to determine how high they were willing to bid on an object.

Before long, most of the items had been sold. We had not bought anything. Finally, I bid on a used oven-range and won it for $10. There were some six-foot long Formica tables on which they had placed some of the goods being auctioned, and these were auctioned last. We watched several tables go for fairly high prices, and we just laid in wait until all those who were anxious to get a table had bid through the roof for them. Then, when there were only two tables left, I started bidding on them and won the bid at $5 for each table.

We loaded all three items into our trailer and headed home. As we drove, I told Blake that I had just spent $20 on some items, and if he wanted to buy one of them from me for what I had paid, he could do so. Then, he could try to sell them at our garage sale the next week. Blake jumped at the chance and said that he wanted one of the tables. I told him to pay me $5 as soon as he got home and the table would be his. I also told him that if he cleaned up my table and the oven-range, he would not be charged for his share of the gas that it took to get to and from the auction. He agreed and we had a deal.

As soon as we got home, he paid me the $5 and then cleaned everything up. We took the oven-range to a used appliance dealer and sold it for $20. Then, we anxiously waited all week to see if anyone would buy our tables at our upcoming weekend garage sale.

Finally, Saturday came and we displayed our tables in the front yard. We put a price tag of $25 on each table. They sold in no time flat. So, one week after Blake handed over the $5, I returned $25 to him. He made a $20 profit. He was thrilled. I was thrilled.

However, we gained more than money from that experience. We had a fun outing, just the two of us, and Blake learned some things about the business world. He learned that you pay for things up front. He learned how to clean things up to make them presentable for resale. And you should have seen him negotiate with the person who bought his table!

Party Store Auction

One day, a neighborhood specialty store went out of business and they held a huge auction to sell their entire inventory. I took some of the kids and we got there early to inspect everything. We wanted to buy it all, of course, but we knew we had to choose only the best lots.

We ended up winning several bids. One included an entire display rack of specialty jumbo balloons with greetings on them, like Happy Birthday, Happy Anniversary and so on. We got over one hundred 4-packs of balloons for a total of $15. Each pack had a list price of $3.95. Later, we sold them all for $1 each and made more than seven times our money back!

We also bought a rack of over 100 greeting cards, most of which were Valentine's Day cards. We made a similar profit on these, but we didn't sell them all so we kept some of the cards for future sales. The following Valentine's Day, I got one out, signed a yellow sticky note, and stuck it inside. Then, I gave it to Joyce. Each year, Joyce gets it out as part of our Valentine decorations. Maybe she is reminding me to never pull that one again!

Bakery Auction

Finally, the day came to take Joyce to an auction. There was a bakery that was going out of business, and everything had to go. We fought the crowd on this one. Since the bakery had just quit doing business two days before the auction, there were lots of fresh baked goods for sale, as well as all of the store's equipment.

We watched for a while as others bid on various items, and then it was our turn. Much of what we bought was for our own kitchen and Joyce's business, but we got such a good deal on some items that we stocked up, planning to resell them. Here's a list of some of the items we purchased:

Item	Number	Cost
stainless steel bowls	13	$10
8" round cake pans	15	$2
shelf-full of baked goods	a lot!	$10
shelf-full of supplies	a ton!	$5

The shelf-full of baked goods that we bought for $10 included 5-gallon buckets of things like chocolate chips, macaroon mix, powdered sugar, and brown sugar. The shelf-full of supplies included plastic cake decorations for each season of the year. When we counted them, they totaled 512 dozen decorations! When we got home, we sorted them into groups of two dozen and put them in sandwich bags. Later, they sold like hotcakes for $0.50 per bag. We made $128 off these items alone—and we only spent $5 plus the cost of the sandwich bags!

We also bought lots of pre-cut wax paper that you put under a cake when you bake it. Joyce was so excited about the bowls, pans and ingredients, and all the rest of the items we purchased, that she never complained again when I mentioned going to another auction!

By the way, we also bought about 1,000 doilies of every size that day. Ten years and three weddings later, we still have lots of doilies. Do you want some?

Bank Auction

Do you remember when several savings & loans and other banks were falling like flies? We remember it well. When this happened, they auctioned off their furniture. I always got there early. There were always many nice, expensive desk and chair sets. There were also computers and cabinets and tables and decorations of every kind. Bankers did believe in luxury!

I bid on several items but didn't win. I was up against the professional office supply stores, and they knew value when they saw it. They also knew when to quit and let the public run the price way up. I watched these dealers to learn how to bid. And soon, I won the bid on a bank president's desk.

The desk was six feet by three feet and made of cherry. It had locks and fancy drawers and looked like new. It had a retail price of $8,000 when it was brand new. I got it for $200. Next, I won the bid on an 18 foot long cherry conference table that was all one piece. It had two pieces of 9' long glass that went on top, and it sat on three huge brass pedestals. The original retail price had been over $15,000. I got it for $195. I bought some other things and then had to hire a moving van to get the pieces home.

We put the desk in my office and started using it right away, but the only room in our home that would hold the huge conference table was the garage, so it was out with the cars and in with the table. When we placed an ad in the paper, we didn't have any luck. We were initially asking $2,000 for the table, but after a couple of weeks of no calls, we reduced it to $1,500.

While we waited for a buyer for the table, we decorated the garage with some fake plants and other items, and then held a formal dinner party for 16 couples. All 32 of us fit around the table, and we enjoyed a fun evening of dining.

Finally, we got a call from a man who owned a construction company. He came to look at the table and offered us $750 for it. We took it. He handed me a check and then we looked at the truck he had brought. It only had a nine-foot bed. He had planned to take four feet out of the middle of the table anyway so that it would fit in his room. So, he asked if we had a circular saw. Soon, he was on top of the table cutting it in half while I stood by, holding the check, when all of a sudden, he hit a steel rod that was in the wood to give it strength. It ruined the saw blade, but more than that, it cast a great fear in our minds that he might back out of buying the table—and now it had a large gash in the middle of it.

I looked at the check and it appeared worthless unless I acted fast. We called our neighbor to come over with his tools and cut the table in half. He had a special blade that could cut through steel, so he came and finished the job. As we loaded the table onto the truck, it was raining, so we loaned the buyer some wool blankets to cover the table with. As he drove away, we wondered if the check would bounce. It didn't, and he even brought our blankets back.

We eventually sold the desk for $500 (without incident). We also had many cabinets and bookcases that kept the kids busy. We let them buy the items, set the price, negotiate with potential buyers, and profit from the sales. It was a great experience for all of them.

Photo # 15: Have you ever seen a gorgeous 18-foot cherry wood table cut in half?

Military Auctions

Every six months, the military bases held auctions. I took several kids to one of these, and we were there early, as usual. We bought a half palette of used green duffle bags for $25. When we got home, we counted them and found at least 100 that were good enough for resale.

The stores were selling them for $12.95 apiece at that time, so we sold ours for $5 each and made 20 times our investment. We also bought some IBM Selectric typewriters and sold them at a good profit as well. Another great find consisted of 11 solid oak bookcases that were four feet wide with three shelves each. We paid $100 for all of them. We kept a couple and sold the rest for $25 each. One of the kids was smart and got in on that deal!

Hardware Store Auction

When I heard that a local hardware store was going out of business, I took off work early and drove the to site. There were lots of new tools being auctioned, but the public bid them up way too high. Finally, they got to the trays full of new nuts and bolts. There were about 50 trays, each five feet long with compartments full of every kind of nut, bolt and washer. Each tray must have weighed 50 pounds. I bid on most of them and won nine trays for a total price of $100. Then, I had to load them in the van without the kids' help!

When I got home, the kids were more than happy to sort through them all and take inventory. We had over $1,600 worth of these products. Since each bin had the retail price of the items marked on it, we set all the trays out each week at our garage sales, and our neighbors enjoyed getting 50% off the retail price. Soon, we had made our money back—and a handsome profit to boot. We still have about 75% of these in our garage today, and they've come in handy.

Tool Auction

One hot summer day, we attended a tool auction. There were several good used tools and workbenches displayed, and toward the end of the auction, I bought a steel workbench that was three feet deep and six feet long. The steel top alone would have cost $200. I got it for $15 and could have had up to 12 more for the same price. I only bought one and kicked myself all the way home for not buying more. I have turned down some mighty nice offers for that bench over the years, but we still use it for our welding projects. Many of the cabinets, workbenches and tables in our workshop have come from auctions. The kids know this, and when the time comes for them to set up their own garages, they know how to do it for much less than paying retail prices!

Dionne's Auction

When I took Dionne to her first auction, we waited all morning without bidding on anything. Finally, the last lot was put up for bid. It consisted of an old car axle, some other scrap steel, and two nice kitchen chairs. The bidding went as follows:

> Auctioneer: Who will give me $50?
> Auctioneer: Who will give me $25?
> Auctioneer: Who will give me $20?
> Auctioneer: Who will give me $15?
> Auctioneer: Who will give me $10?
> Auctioneer: Who will give me $5?
> Auctioneer: Who will give me $2.50?

At this point, Dionne nudged me and said, louder than she anticipated, "Dad!"

The auctioneer and the entire crowd heard her and they all looked at me, so I spoke up and said, "I guess we'll give $2.50 for it."

Auctioneer: "Sold!"

Dionne knew that this was hers, and she was excited to see what would happen with her new purchase. We took everything and loaded it up into the trailer. We did not want the axle or scrap steel at home, so before we left the auction, we called a scrap steel dealer and found out what they would pay per pound. We stopped by there on the way home and unloaded the axle and all of the steel. They paid $5 for it.

At this point, Dionne had made all of her money back and then some—and she still had two nice chairs. She cleaned them up the next week and sold the pair for $25. She had invested $2.50 and came away with $30, but the gains were not only financial ones that day. We had fun doing it together—and we will never forget that fateful nudge.

Chapter 5—Faith and Trust

Most of the problems in the world today would no longer exist if man would learn to trust (or love) his fellow man. Many of these problems result from parents teaching their children ways in which to "not trust" others.

How many keys do we have on our key chains? How many PINs and passwords do we have? How thick are the walls at the bank? How many of us will pick up a hitchhiker today? Perhaps some of these precautions are necessary today in order to provide for our own security. However, if we have opportunities to step outside of this paradigm and trust someone, we should do so. We need to let our kids be involved so they can see the wonderful feeling we get when we extend our trust.

The stories in this chapter relate some of our experiences of trusting others, both inside and outside of our family. The end result has always been wonderful for us and for our kids.

A Cooler with a Sign and a Shoebox

When we lived in Arizona, we had a large garden, and we really enjoyed all of the food that it produced. Each year, we planted 150 tomato plants. At the time, we had nine children, and each got to vote every year as to whether or not they wanted to be involved in the garden project. We usually got the seven oldest to participate. We took the cost of the garden out of their savings accounts, and they did all of the work in the garden. Then, they split the money earned from selling tomatoes.

Because we used black plastic over the garden to keep out the weeds, and a drip watering system—their work only consisted of tilling, planting and harvesting. The tomatoes have always done very well, and the kids would sell them for $2 for a brown lunch bag full. People always love a good homegrown tomato.

For several years, we had a few of the smaller kids stand out on the busy street near our home with a cooler full of tomatoes, a huge beach umbrella, and a couple of signs to wave at the cars as they drove by. They always sold all of the tomatoes that we produced. Two years in a row, a picture of our kids selling tomatoes appeared on the front page of our local newspaper. The article described their business.

One year, we were all too busy on one particular day to sell the tomatoes on the street, so we put the bags in a cooler on the front porch. We put a sign beside them that listed the price, and then put a shoebox beside the cooler for the money. Then, we went away for the day. When we returned, all of the tomatoes were gone, and the shoebox was full of money.

The money was more than enough to pay for all of the tomatoes, but the added bonus was all the notes we found in the shoebox from various customers. They thanked us for trusting them, and a couple even left us a tip.

We sat our kids down and told them that we were not as interested in selling tomatoes as we were in teaching them to work hard, be honest, and to love (trust) their neighbors. We felt that this experience was a good way for all of us to learn to trust our fellow man. From that day on, we always sold our tomatoes on the front porch from an unattended cooler with a sign and a shoebox—whether we were at home or not. And we often got tips and special little notes. In a world where nations point missiles at each other and issue vicious threats, we are glad to have the opportunity to teach the next generation the way it ought to be.

New Growth

In 1988, there were some huge forest fires in Yellowstone National Park. A large percent of the park was burned. We have been back there a couple of times since the fires occurred, and the sight would have been very sad—if we would have let it.

I loved Yellowstone so much that I didn't want to remember it all burned up. So, when we returned in 2000, I had our digital camera with me, and I tried to take pictures of the area that would make me appreciate the fires of Yellowstone.

As we drove through the park, we noticed huge sections where tall lodge pole pine trees stood with no branches on them. The burned trees were dead, and this left an obvious negative view that most people probably took home with them. However, I noticed that near the base of the standing dead trees, there was a twelve-year-old forest of bright green. These were brand new trees doing their best to catch up with their ancestors in height and stature. I took many pictures of these smaller, next generation trees in various stages of their development.

I related the growth and progress of the young trees to the growth and progress of the children that we are trusted with today. Not that we are a bunch of old burned out lodge pole pines, but the analogy works. You see, the lodge pole pine has two kinds of pinecones. One kind falls off the tree, and when it opens up on the ground, a new tree is born. The other kind falls off the tree and lies dormant on the forest floor until it is opened up by severe heat, as is the case when there is a forest fire.

We were seeing trees from the latter kind of pinecone as the new forest was developing in Yellowstone. I explained this to the family, and we came away with good memories of Yellowstone that year. We didn't focus on the fact that so much of it had burned, but that it was healing and progressing as designed. It was a good reminder that life is what you make it.

Pure Trust

Back when I was in the process of reading the journal of Lewis and Clark at lunchtime each day, I would come home and share the stories that I read with our family. One story that I have told many times is about when Lewis and Clark (and their expedition) reached the end of the Missouri River and had to climb the mountains. They bought some ponies from some Indians for the trip. When they reached the other side of the mountains and found some new rivers to follow westward, they built canoes and no longer needed their ponies. However, since they planned to return one year later, they really wanted to keep the horses. They were faced with a dilemma.

Coincidentally, they had just met a new tribe of Indians, so they asked the Indians if they could leave their ponies there for a year, and then retrieve them when they returned. The Indians agreed. So, Lewis and Clark went on to the Pacific and wintered near present day Portland, Oregon. The next year, on their return trip, they found that all of their ponies were alive and well and waiting for them. That is an incredible story of trust about the American Indian that is not taught in school. It is, however, taught in our home.

On one occasion, our family joined a wagon train in Bayard, Nebraska. The plan was for everyone to hike or ride in wagons each day. At the end of the day, a school bus would arrive with drivers for the support vehicles (such as horse trailers, motor homes, etc.) so they could move them forward.

The day we arrived, a lot of other people did too. When the leader of the wagon train saw my 15-passenger van, he asked if I would transport the drivers to the next town the following day. I agreed. Then, he said that there was a catch. I would be hiking the 23 miles to the next town, but my van needed to be there when I arrived. He said that he had found a local resident who volunteered to drive my van on ahead while I hiked, and then asked if I would mind giving him my keys.

My first thought went back to what I had read about Lewis and Clark, about how they had trusted the Indians whom they had just met. I handed him the keys. Everything worked out well and our family grew that day because we trusted our fellow man.

Commitment

There have been times when one of the kids has come to me wanting something. I usually make sure that they completely understand the terms by which they will receive it. In these situations, a little humor can provide a lasting memory.

For example, if Capri wants to stay up late to watch a movie (even though watching movies is a rarity in our home)—I will tell her that she can only after the following has happened:

I say, "Stand up and put your left hand on your right ear."

She does.

I say, "Put your left foot in the air."

She does.

I say, "Put the index finger of your right hand on your left knee."

She does.

I say, "Tilt your head to the left."

She does.

I say, "Twist your mouth crooked."

She does.

I say, "Repeat after me: I, Capri Clifton…"

She says, "I, Capri Clifton…"

I continue, "…want to stay up late tonight to watch a movie."

She continues, "…want to stay up late tonight to watch a movie."

I continue, "If you let me do this, I will get up on time tomorrow…"

She continues, "If you let me do this, I will get up on time tomorrow…"

I conclude, "…and make my bed without being asked."

She concludes, "…and make my bed without being asked."

Permission is granted and Capri resumes a normal posture. After going through all of this, she is not too likely to forget what she agreed to do. This has been effective to help kids remember when they have made a commitment, while providing some humor at the same time. Being a parent can be great fun.

Difference Between a Bad and a Good Haircut

When I met Joyce, she already knew how to cut her brothers' hair. So, once we had sons, she would routinely cut their hair. The boys have loved it. Some of them are grown now, and they have probably never been inside a barbershop. But this tradition did not stop there.

Joyce has taught the boys and their sisters how to cut a boy's hair. Whenever a friend needs a haircut, they usually have one of our kids give them one. Dionne gives Matt, Connor and Spencer haircuts. Amy cuts Trevor's hair while he holds the mirror so he can watch her, and Trevor has starting cutting Ethan's hair. Tanya cuts Logan's hair, and Trent will let any of his older siblings cut his hair.

Over the decades, there have been a few hairs cut that ought not to have been. However, no tears have ever been shed because our family's motto has always been: "The difference between a bad haircut and a good haircut is about two weeks."

Photo # 16: Trevor learning to cut Blake's hair.

Be Prepared

One night, we held a special Family Counsel to prepare a 72-hour kit (see glossary) for each member of the family. We had bought everyone a backpack and had spent weeks collecting the things that we wanted to put in each kit. Since this was a serious effort with significant cost involved, we were anxious to only put what was necessary in each person's kit.

At our special Family Counsel, we would hold up an item and ask who would like one of them (or some of them) in their kit. Some things were not optional, but perhaps the quantity was. There were flashlights, batteries, food, shelter, clothing, space blankets, first aid kits, sewing kits, and much more. We appreciate the fact that we had raised some very thrifty kids, and that they were being diligent to only request items that they thought they would need.

So, when we held up the 12-hour glow sticks and asked how many each child wanted, the responses were very slow in coming in. Finally, Dacia (who was 10 at the time) said that she wanted eight of them. This was a huge request because we were building more than a dozen bags. Everyone laughed at her and let her know that she did not need that many glow sticks.

Just then, all of the lights in the house went out for a few seconds. This startled everyone, and as soon as lights came back on *everyone* suddenly wanted eight glow sticks too!

I Promise

In order to emphasize the importance of keeping a promise, we have reserved the word "promise" to be very special. In our family, if you say that word, it means that you will do whatever you promise, without fail. This is very useful in teaching children to be honest.

One day, I approached our 3 year-old daughter and told her that if she put her arms way up in the air, I *promised* I would *not* tickle her. She put her arms high in the air, and even though I slowly moved my hands toward her, she never wavered. Her hands remained high in the sky. She completely trusted her Dad because he had "promised."

On another occasion, Dacia (who was 9 at the time) was on a committee to raise funds for her school so they could buy a new tree. She had the opportunity on two different occasions to make public announcements concerning the matter. Unknown to us at the time, on both occasions, she chickened out.

Finally, the day came for her to go to the City Council with the teacher and some other students and ask them to help raise the money. Her teacher let us know that she had been too scared to talk in front of a group prior to this event. However, she really wanted to go to the City Council meeting. So, I had a nice discussion with her that resulted in her "promise" to talk that night if she was allowed to go to the meeting. She could not chicken out.

She promised, and then went to that town meeting. When it was her turn to speak, she began by saying, "Mr. Mayor and City Council, we are from…" She ended up delivering a wonderful address and had all the confidence in the world doing so—because she had made a "promise."

Internet Usage Standards

The Internet is a distinctive two-sided coin. On one side, it can be a great tool that can be used to accomplish many good things related to business, education, shopping, entertainment, family life and communication. On the other side of the coin, it can be misused to extremes that lead the user down some mighty dark paths of inappropriate behavior, and possibly even criminal acts.

Why would we want such a device within the walls of our home if it has the potential for such destructive power? Well, Joyce and I decided that we would rather teach our children about the good things the Internet can provide, and then make our children aware that it also possess bad things that they should avoid.

To accomplish this, we came up with an "Internet Usage Standards" rule. Each year, we modify it as needed. Then, we print it out and hold a special Home Night and discuss the many ways in which we may use the Internet in our lives—whether at home, at work, at school or at play. During this meeting, we point out the many good uses of the Internet. We recognize that when kids go off to college today, the professor is very likely to have them log onto the Internet to retrieve data, do research, create documents, and even submit their assignments. Similarly, many of today's jobs require workers to use computers and the Internet. Therefore, learning to use the Internet properly at home is good training for what lies ahead at school and at work.

At the end of these annual family meetings, we each sign our Internet Usage Standards document and commit to the rules of usage that we have discussed. A copy is then posted next to every computer in the house. One of the reasons that we review and sign it each year is that the Internet is changing all the time. There are always new, devious ways in which people are tricked into visiting areas that they should not. We change this document and make new commitments accordingly. Another reason we sign it each year is that it serves as a good reminder that we have each made a commitment as to our conduct in using the Internet—even if we use a computer outside of the home. It also gives us a chance to clear up any misunderstandings that may have arisen. Finally, it helps to teach the younger kids (who are just beginning to use the Internet) what the family rules are on Internet usage.

We do not allow our children to have computers in their bedrooms or other places where there is not public access. This also helps to keep conduct on the computer at a level that is consistent with our family standards. We also do not allow chatting with strangers on the Internet. When our kids were little, we taught them to never talk to strangers. That concept applies more than ever now that the Internet is here.

We do not have anything against Internet filters which are designed to restrict access to inappropriate sites. Overall, they will not harm your computer and, in fact, they will catch and filter many things that you do not want on your computer. And what can be wrong with anything that cleans up smut? Unfortunately, however, when you use such programs, they may filter some legitimate, useful information as well. Besides, if you think that any program like that can filter out everything that is undesirable, think again! Nothing can possibly be all-inclusive in filtering out smut. It would be a never-ending battle as it would never be current. Also, the biggest drawback to these programs is that they can give parents a false sense of security. There is no way that we would install one and then sit back and worry any less about the Internet being used improperly in our home. Whether we filter or not, our kids still need to be *taught* the dangers of using the Internet.

There are some who profess that we should not allow the Internet into our home at all. On the surface, this may seem to hold some wisdom. However, we feel that we cannot go through life sheltering our children, or run along behind them with a pillow, ready to catch each one when they fall. We cannot and will not always be there. Therefore, we need to teach our children right from wrong, and how to govern themselves.

There are many other modern conveniences whose use can lead to negative influences—including the telephone; movies and videos; cable, satellite and even regular network TV; CD and DVD players, tape players, automobiles, and so on. If we were to remove all of these things from our homes, could we really relax knowing our kids were safe from their bad influences? The answer is "No!" Anywhere they go in life, they can be exposed to these things, whether it is at a neighbor's home, at school, at the public library, or at a multitude of other places.

It is simply best to *teach* your children about the good and the bad, and to help them understand how important it is to always avoid the bad. Then, it is equally important to give them the freedom to grow, and to show your trust that they will keep those commitments.

By being honest with our children, guiding them, and staying close to them—we have been able to discuss such issues openly. And hopefully, they will keep the commitments that they have made.

Early to Bed, Early to Rise

When our oldest kids were quite young, we adopted the habit of *not* sleeping in. We would put our young kids to bed at 8:00 p.m., and they would go right to sleep. In the morning, we would get them up at 6:00 a.m.

One night, we had some guests over. When it was bedtime, the kids came into the room to say goodnight. Our guests asked what time we got our kids up each morning. Joyce told them. Then, one guest asked, "How do you get them up at 6:00 a.m.?" Joyce replied, "We put them to bed at 8:00 p.m." The guest looked a little confused for a moment, and then asked, "Well, how do you get them to bed at 8:00 p.m.?" Joyce replied, "We get them up at 6:00 a.m."

State Champs and A New Baby

When Carmin and Monica were in high school, they were the statisticians for the men's basketball team one year. As a result, they went to all of the games and were part of the team. That year, their team had some great players, and they wound up in the Arizona State High School Basketball Championships, which was played in the same arena that the Phoenix Suns used. This was a thrill for them!

The morning of the big game, we held a special Family Council to announce that we were expecting Shayla in the fall. We met in the basement of our home, and then I got out the family gavel and called the meeting to order. I started out by asking if anyone knew why we were meeting, and they all said, "Is Mom having another baby?" Well, that made it a short meeting, and after confirming their suspicions and providing a few details, the meeting was adjourned. Everyone was excited to welcome child #10 into our family.

That evening, the basketball team lived up to everyone's expectations and won a hard fought game to become state champs. Carmin and Monica were on cloud nine as they walked out of the arena. Becky, who is a very close family friend, had a son on the team. She caught up with our girls and walked with them toward the parking lot. Monica said, "This is a great day in my life." Becky said, "Yes, it's not everyday that you win the state championship in basketball." Monica then replied, "No, this is a great day because we won the state championship in basketball and my mom is going to have another baby!" Carmin agreed wholeheartedly.

When Becky later told us this story, we were thrilled. It was a joy to be the parents of kids who loved their siblings.

Friends On Shore First

During the summers of my college years, I worked as a lifeguard and taught swimming lessons. Over the years, I have probably taught over 1,000 people how to swim, including those who were mentally or physically challenged. Many of the people I taught were adults, and it seemed that the older the students were, the more fear of the water they had. This was especially true if they had ever had a bad experience in the water. Their fear was often immeasurable.

I knew that I could teach these prospective swimmers some skills if I could get them in the water. I also knew, however, that to them, the water represented a place they did not want to be. They did not feel safe

in the water. I knew that they could perform as
would need to trust me in the water in order to
accomplishment. In order for them to gain confid‹   ‒, ı spent
time with each one on shore, gaining his or her trust. I kept telling them
that I had a secret for them. They would come close and listen as I whispered, "I'm your friend, and I won't let anything bad happen to you in
the water, trust me."

I repeated this many times. When I finally got them in the water, I
would tell them that I had a secret for them. They would instantly
remember that I was their friend, and that I would not let anything bad
happen to them while they were in the water. They knew they could
trust me. My plan worked. In no time, they would start swimming!
Soon, they gained their own confidence and did not need to lean on me
anymore.

Life is like swimming. We need to find those whom we can trust—
whether on the shore or in the water. And it is so important to gain the
trust of your child during normal times (on the shore) so that when a
potentially dangerous situation arises (in the water), they will know
that they can trust you and that you will not let them down.

A Roomy House

In 1985, I took a temporary consulting job in Naperville, Illinois that
lasted two wonderful years. We kept our home in Arizona and arranged
to have someone live there while we were away. We took very little with
us in the way of furniture or belongings of any kind. Each of the seven
kids had a mattress, but no box spring. We took our king size bed; two
folding tables; one computer; one sewing machine; some dishes; ten
folding chairs; clothes; and our seven kids, ranging in age from 2 to 11.

Before we moved, I had tried for weeks to find someone who would
rent to a family with seven kids. In some towns, there were laws that did

not allow more than a certain number of kids in an apartment. I was getting desperate. Finally, I found a man who would rent an unfurnished house to us. It had four bedrooms, a kitchen, a living room, a dinning room, 2 full baths and a half bath, and an unfinished basement. It was in a very nice part of town with lots of kids in the neighborhood. There was even a neighborhood pond that was perfect for ice-skating when it froze in the winter. I told him I'd take it.

We moved our few belongings into the home, and it still looked empty! We had no furniture, and you could literally see from one end of the house to the other. However, we were not ashamed of it, as we were determined to make this a great experience for our family.

One day, a neighbor lady came to visit Joyce and commented on how spacious our home was. She lived in a house with the very same floor plan down the street, and she didn't think that hers was as roomy. Joyce jokingly told her to go home and get rid of all of her furniture and her house would be roomy too.

Our kids had spent most, if not all, of their lives living in the same home. Therefore, they had never been "the new kid on the block." Since we moved in October, they had to leave one school and move to another. This can be challenging for a child. Dionne was the first to meet a neighbor girl her own age, and soon, the other kids found their own friends. They did a great job of adjusting.

When Joyce went for a walk one day with Trent in the stroller, she passed by a house that had just disposed of some huge boxes. She couldn't resist. I wish we had a picture of her pushing that stroller while pulling two huge boxes several blocks back to our house. It was a feat, but she made it, and we were all excited to have something with which to fill up our house. The kids played with these boxes for hours, just crawling in and out of them.

Christmas was coming and we had already told the kids that they would not be receiving very many gifts because we did not have room to take anything extra back to Arizona. They were all okay with this. Soon they began making plans.

The girls, led by Dionne, started constructing a fort out of one of the boxes. They planned to give to the boys for Christmas. They made it look like a real fort and kept it hidden so the boys wouldn't see it until Christmas Day. The boys, led by Trevor, were busy making the other box into a playhouse for the girls! It had curtains covering the cutout windows, cardboard shelves for dolls, and even a fully functional garage door. It was also kept a secret so that the girls wouldn't see their present until Christmas Day.

As Christmas approached, each group was so excited to give their gift to the others that they did not even talk about what they wanted for Christmas. They had made other homemade gifts that year as well, and they were anxious to give them to each other.

On Christmas morning, excitement filled the air as the boys were blindfolded and led to where their gift had been constructed and hidden away. They were all surprised. It was just what they wanted. Then, they anxiously led the blindfolded girls to where their new playhouse was. The girls were thrilled with it, and they were surprised to find that all of their dolls had been placed in the dollhouse at the last minute.

It brought tears to the eyes of their parents to see how content they could be with such simple gifts. Our children taught us a great lesson that day. Their homemade offerings had put an emphasis on *giving* gifts, rather than receiving them.

Another surprise came in the way of a phone call that we received the day after Christmas that year. It was from a neighbor who wanted to know if her kids could come over to our house to play. She said that she wasn't sure why they wanted to come over, since she had given them many really nice, expensive toys for Christmas, but they did. All they wanted to do was to come over and play in our cardboard boxes (a.k.a. fort and playhouse). Happiness is often derived from simplicity.

Overcoming Fears

Like many people, Monica does not like bugs. When she was a young girl, we were staying at the family cabin in the mountains of Arizona. There are many bugs in the mountains, and the cabin bathroom always seemed to attract daddy longlegs. These are harmless spiders, but they do tickle when they crawl on you.

Monica avoided using the bathroom as much as possible. I did not think that this was healthy, so I came up with a plan. I told her that I would pay her $0.10 for every daddy longlegs that she would pick up by the leg and put into a jar. After much coaching from her siblings, she managed to get 11 of them into the jar, and I paid her $1.10. But she gained more than money that day. She gained the confidence that she could overcome her fears.

Years later, Dacia was running away from a cockroach. I offered her a reward if she would pick it up and bring it to me. She did, I paid, and she had overcome her fear as well.

In both these cases, neither child was forced to participate in something that they did not want to participate in. All I did was provide enough incentive that all of a sudden they wanted to do it. These were simple fears, but the conquering of them can translate to more difficult fears later on. The theory is the same. Find enough incentive to set the fear aside and conquer it.

Sportsmanship

In almost every sporting contest, someone wins and someone loses. It's part of the game to have a winner, and it's also part of the game to have a loser. Far too often, people think that their team has to win every game. I have tried to teach the kids that there is nothing wrong with losing a game, although they should try hard to win, fair and square.

I think that it is far more important to learn how to lose than how to win. Anybody can, and does, win with a happy heart. We have tried to teach our kids that when they lose, they need to do so with a happy heart as well. Since life is full of winning and losing situations, we need to be gracious winners when we win, as well as gracious losers when we lose.

When I coached a youth baseball team, I had two kinds of players trying out for the same position. There was the player who did not have all the natural athletic abilities but was a hustler. Then there was the natural athlete who sat back and coasted, not fully applying himself. When the hustler missed a ground ball, he would hurry after it and come up throwing it to the proper base. He tried to make up for his mistake as quickly and as thoroughly as possible. However, when the natural athlete missed a ground ball, he threw his glove down in disgust. He did not know how to accept defeat. In the long run, the hustler made the better player because he seemed to carry the team more when times got tough. How I would have loved to have had a team full of naturally gifted athletes who were *also* hustlers!

Since those days, we have tried to apply the same concept to raising our kids. We have tried to make sure that they have had both winning and losing situations in life, as well as in sports. When those special moments came after they had lost at something, we would have a discussion and try to find the good in all that had happened to them. This can be a challenge, but it can also be quite rewarding. There is good in all that happens to us. Our job is to find that good and magnify it so that it overshadows the gloom of defeat.

Dating

The subject of dating can scare parents and youth alike. But it doesn't have to be that way. In our home, the children do not date until they are 16 years old. From the time the kids were little, we made them aware of this. They have accepted this in much the same way that they have accepted that they will not be able to drive until they are 16.

However, the year that Trevor turned 16, the Homecoming dance was on his birthday. He wanted to go, but for some reason, he had not asked anyone to the dance. Finally, I pulled him aside and said that it was okay to ask a girl to the dance, since he would be officially 16 when the day arrived. Perhaps because of that conversation, he asked a nice young lady to Homecoming and had an enjoyable first date.

When the children turn 16, they are encouraged to only to go on multiple couple dates. This has worked out well. We don't encourage going steady. They will have lots of time later to settle down with someone. We feel that in high school, it is best to go out with a lot of different kids. We have found that when rules such as these are understood and anticipated in advance, they don't seem so threatening.

We also have a curfew. The older kids must be home by midnight, or call by then if there is a problem. They let us know where they will be for the evening, and if that changes, they are to call and let us know. We have voice mail on our phone, and more than once, late at night, we have been on the phone when the child who is out on a date has tried to call. They simply left a message and all was well. Cell phones can come in handy here too, as there have been times when we have sent the family cell phone along on the date.

Our kids have gone on a fair amount of "group dates." These are activities where young men and young women go in large groups. They are not necessarily paired up, and in fact, there is not always an equal number of girls and boys. They have all enjoyed some great memories from these kinds of dates

Through the years, we have witnessed some mighty creative ways in which to ask someone out. One night, for instance, the doorbell rang. When we answered it, nobody was there. However, lying on the door-mat was a cherry pie for Carmin. She had been dreaming that a certain young man might ask her to the big dance. Now, here was this pie with her name on it, but she had no idea who it was from.

The whole family gathered around and the camera was rolling. We helped her eat the pie to find out which special someone had asked her. When we discovered the benefactor's name inside the pie, Carmin was thrilled. If he had just called her up, it wouldn't have been nearly as much fun!

Chapter 6—Goals

If you don't know where you're going and how you're going to get there, perhaps your life has no direction or purpose. If parents don't set goals for themselves and for their kids, how can they be sure of the family's final destination? If you have read this far in this book, you obviously care about the next generation. Make sure that you teach them (by example first) how to set and achieve goals so their lives will not drift aimlessly by. As these stories will show, all goals, regardless of their magnitude, are achieved one step at a time. Make sure your kids learn this valuable lesson.

Jar On the Mantle Yields A Bald One That Soars

In our family, participating in scouting is very important and enjoyable. On each boy's 8th, 9th and 10th birthdays, he gets the appropriate Cub Scout book and uniform for the upcoming year. On his 11th birthday, he gets a Boy Scout Handbook and a new uniform.

Also on each of these birthdays, each boy gets a gift that he can open—but only part way because it is in a jar. He is not to open the jar until he has met his next rank advancement. The jar sits on the mantle of the fireplace to remind us all of his goals in scouting, and that we can all help him.

He can hold the jar at any time, but he cannot remove the lid until the next rank has been earned. The gift inside the jar is always something relating to the great program of scouting—such as a pocketknife, a compass, a flint and steel fire starter kit, or a backpack and frame. Okay…you might be wondering how we got a backpack and frame into a one-quart jar. We didn't. We bought the pack and allowed the child see it, but not touch it. We then put a note in the jar that described the backpack in detail.

As parents, we have been very much involved in scouting by supporting many Cub Scout and Boy Scout activities. Our three sons have each earned his Eagle at the age of 12. And each has several Eagle Palms, which represent advancement beyond the Eagle level. To us, it is important for a young man to get his Eagle early. When he turns 14, things start to get in the way of scouting—such as a social life, dances, and high school sports. When he turns 16, dating and driving often take the place of scouting. By the time he turns 18, it's too late to participate. A boy that is 11, 12 or 13 has more time than ever—and they are very capable of earning the rank of Eagle. However, it does take an active involvement by loving parents to assist the young man and the scout leaders. The rewards are worth the efforts of all.

Photo # 17: Blake gets a pocketknife in a jar for his 8th birthday.

The Origin of Our Pulley Swing

One summer, our family took a vacation that included visiting relatives in Idaho who lived on a farm. While we were there, we got to see and use the homemade zip line that they had constructed between two trees. For those of you who don't know, a zip line is a strong cable with a pulley on it that is connected above the ground between two points. You can hang on to a bar attached to a chain that is connected to the pulley, and then jump off a high ledge to zoom across the yard. It was fun to ride, and our kids wanted one at our Arizona home. I told them that someday we would build one, and then I forgot about it. They did not.

The first day after we got back home, I came home from work to find that the kids had built a zip line. I asked where they got the materials. They said that we had everything they needed in the garage. I knew how limited the zip line supplies were in the garage, so I dropped everything to go see what they had. They had taken some 16-gauge speaker wire and connected it between the swing set and a citrus tree as it crossed over the trampoline. On the cable, they had attached a very small pulley. Attached to the pulley was a piece of string that was tied around an old set of bicycle handlebars that they intended to hold onto as they zoomed across the yard in the air.

In seconds, I could see that this situation was no safer than square dancing on the freeway! I had to admire their desire and ingenuity, but they had some real problems with stability. They had ridden it a few times and said that it really worked. I asked them to take it down before someone got hurt and I said that we would design and build a real zip line—but one that was actually a pulley swing.

We went inside and drew out a plan. They each added their own ideas, and soon, we had a monster of a pulley swing planned. I took the plans to work the next day. Several hardware and software engineers each added to the design. Soon, the plan was finalized and it was time to build and install our contraption. I told the kids that they had to help pay for it, so we found some way for them to raise money. It took about three full Saturdays to build it, and then we were ready to try it out. The design was as follows:

The Pulley Swing Design

We bought a 5/8" thick cable that was rated for about 2,000 pounds and an equally large and strong pulley. From the pulley, we extended two chains down to a rubber seat that we got from a swing set. Most zip lines use a handle bar, but we thought that we had better have a place for people to sit safely. We already had a 13 foot tall swing set, so we decided that this could be the termination point. We removed one of the swings and then put up a super strong, drop forged eyebolt to hold the cable 13' off the ground.

For the other end, we had to get a bit more creative. We bought two used 27-foot steel light poles. We drilled the appropriate holes, and then we dug two 4 ½ foot deep holes in the ground about four feet apart. We had to have our neighbor use his pickup truck from his property to pull the poles up into place and let them settle down into their holes. This left the poles sticking 22 ½ feet above the ground. We then made the poles true and secured them with temporary ropes while we mixed and poured in 2,000 pounds of concrete.

After the concrete dried, we rented some scaffolding and a friend came over to help me weld some 1" diameter pipes between the poles as ladder rungs, every 12 inches up the poles. Soon, we had a huge ladder whose rungs went up about 14 feet. We then went to the top of the poles, installed an eyebolt, and connected the cable with the pulley on it. We also welded one more cross bar across the top.

The cable stretched 83 feet across the yard and dropped from a height of 22 ½ feet to 13 feet. This gave it good slope for a fast ride. The person using it "only" had to climb up 14 feet above the ground to reach the swing to sit on. We felt that we had to have two light poles because the leverage on a single pole would cause it to bend too much. We were glad we did. We even hired a professional welder to come and re-weld all of my welds to make sure that the ladder would not fall apart. We had some extra pipe on the backside of the ladder, so we extended it out and hung a 15-foot high climbing rope.

When we were done, we were a long ways from the original zip line the kids had designed and built, but hopefully, they were now much safer. We attached a rope to the pulley so that after riding it, the swing could be pulled back to the next user.

Finally the day came for our first neighborhood party with our new toy. We love to throw parties, so we invited 250 people over for a Labor Day barbeque. About 175 had responded that they would come. We got the yard ready and all was well. The party was to begin at 5:30 p.m. At 5:00 p.m., the skies began to darken and a huge thunderstorm moved in on us. By 5:30, at least two inches of rain had already fallen. Thunder and lighting filled the sky. Immediately, the phone began to ring off the hook. People were calling to ask if we were still going to have the party. We told them that we had figured out a way to barbeque on the covered patio, and that they should come. Over the next hour, we got another three inches of rain, and all the kids in the neighborhood were terribly disappointed that they could not ride the pulley swing.

Then, all of a sudden, it stopped raining. The skies cleared and the kids were all asking me if they could go out and ride it. I told them that we had to wait for the lightning to move away first. I taught everyone how to count the number of seconds between the lightning strikes and the sound of the thunder, then divide by five to determine about how many miles away it was. We had all kinds of math going on that day, and soon it was safe to play in the yard.

By this time, our yard had filled with about a foot of water. It looked just like it did when we flood irrigated! So, off went the shoes and socks. Literally dozens of kids and adults ran out to try our new pulley swing. For the next several hours, there was a line of no less than 20 people waiting to take their turn. The riders enjoyed letting their feet drag through the water to simulate water skiing. Everyone had a blast that day, and I was relieved that we had corrected the original design.

The pulley swing became a major part of our backyard, and it soon became a magnet that attracted all kinds of kids to play at our house. We knew that if our kids had their friends come over to our house to play, we would know where they were and what they were doing. This idea carried over to our next house, the one that we built in Utah and still live in today. It now has a pulley swing too—and folks of all ages have thoroughly enjoyed it.

Photo # 18: Ingenious kids engineer the original pulley swing.

Photo # 19: Clifton Family on the ladder to the pulley swing while Dacia hangs in the air.

We Want a Swing Set

When we moved from Arizona to Utah, we had to leave behind our huge swing set, pulley swing and everything else in our backyard playground. Since we first had to build our house, landscaping and a new playground had to wait. The kids were patient with us for about three years, and then one summer, they asked if they could have a swing set. We told them that they are not free (especially the kind we would build, which would be 15 feet tall and hold several adults swinging on it at the same time). Finally, however, we came up with a project to which they agreed.

We had some leftover glow sticks from a former project that we had not sold. These provide a colored light when you snap them, mixing two chemicals inside together. The Fourth of July was approaching, and we decided that we would take these to the park. There was a huge bowl shaped field where everyone could sit and watch the fireworks being set off at a nearby stadium. We knew that thousands of people would be there. So, the kids thought that they could sell the glow sticks to other kids at a fair price. We told them that we could put all of the money from the sales into the swing set fund.

We got to the site early, and Joyce's sister and her kids came along with us. Our shy daughters joined up with their not-so-shy boy cousins and they were off. For advertising purposes, we gave each kid a glow stick to light and hang around their neck. Soon, we saw several other kids were wearing them. Our kids started walking around the perimeter of the bowl, and as it began to get dark, you could easily tell where they were by the number of other kids wearing glow sticks in the crowd. They sold out and probably could have sold another 200 of them! They brought back a backpack full of money that went to the swing set fund.

Our backyard would not be ready for us to build the swing set until the next summer, but we went ahead and started buying the parts for the swing set to show the kids some kind of progress on our part. So, we designed it, and then went out and bought all the poles, swings, chains and bolts. This held them over until the next spring when we got the landscaping done and built a beautiful swing set.

Raising the money for the swing set was not the only thing the kids took part in. They also got to help with all of the labor…but that is the subject of another story.

Don't Bite Your Nails

Perhaps one of the most common habits that people have is to bite their fingernails. Our family is no different, as some of us bite our fingernails also. In order to encourage our girls to do otherwise, we made a family rule that they could only use fingernail polish on nails that were long enough. We would hold weekly interviews, and the first thing in the interview was to have the kids show me their nails. The girls would run their fingernails down my arm, and if it did not hurt, their nails were too short for polish. Sometimes some nails would qualify for polish and other nails on the same hand would not. The missing nail polish served as a good reminder during the week. This really worked. It kept their minds on the effort all week long. And sometimes, a young child would come to me mid-week and want to scratch my arm to test their nails.

The Origin of the Bakery Business

In the summer of 1987, we were planning on moving from our temporary home in Naperville, Illinois back to our permanent home in Peoria, Arizona. We had seven kids at the time, the oldest of which was 12. We decided that it would be fun to "stop by" Disney World in Orlando, Florida "on our way home." (Yes, even though Orlando is *not* on the way from Naperville to Peoria.)

We checked into the cost and came up with the plan. We wanted to make sure that the kids appreciated the extra fun at Disney World, so we asked them to help raise the money for the price of admission. Joyce immediately led them in baking bread for our neighbors.

First, they learned how to get organized. They decided on some products that would sell, like homemade bread and cinnamon rolls. Then, they contacted the neighbors and got some orders. There was a great response, and they had many orders to fill. More orders came in each week and the kids worked hard and learned a lot. They spent three months baking all they could.

Finally, the time came for the trip home, and we pulled out all of the money from the bank that they had earned and put it into Traveler's Checks. After a few days of driving, we arrived in Orlando. When we went up to the ticket booth and requested a three-day pass for our entire family of nine—plus tickets for each of us to enjoy the luau dinner, the clerk rang up the total. We promptly handed her enough Traveler's Checks to cover the cost. Each child stood there and realized their own part in getting our family into Disney World. This was a trip that we all thoroughly enjoyed, not just because of where we went, but also because of how we got there.

Planning Meals

At the beginning of the summer one year, Joyce mentioned to me that it was becoming difficult to get the kids involved in planning and preparing our evening meals. We came up with the idea that we would hold a Family Council and have the kids help us work out the problem.

We met and listed all of the kinds of foods that we liked for our evening meals. We then asked the kids which ones wanted to help prepare the meals on which days. When a child signed up to help cook on a given evening, they got to specify what we ate that day. We also had a rule that the cooks did not have to do the dishes, which added another incentive. Soon, we had our summer calendar full of names of cooks and the menus for each evening.

This took a lot of pressure off Joyce, and it made shopping much easier, since we knew in advance what we would be eating, and when. If the person in charge of a meal had a last minute conflict, he or she traded with someone else and the meals went on.

The system taught the children responsibility and accountability. Also, they realized that some of their favorite foods were not so delicious if they were hard to prepare. Their entire outlook on kitchen duty changed. And along the way, they did pick up some great cooking and management skills

Skipping Out of Grand Canyon

One year, we took some friends to the Grand Canyon. We planned to hike half way down to the Colorado River to a place called Indian Gardens. This is not an ordinary walk. It is a rough hike of 4 ½ miles each way on the Bright Angel Trail. Although half of the trip is downhill, the other half is *uphill*. Seasoned hikers warn that it will take a person twice as long to hike out of the canyon as it takes to hike into it. With all the information we could gather, we made plans to make the round trip in one day, and away we went.

I had several of the kids along on the hike, including Dacia, who was 2 years old at the time. Joyce stayed on top with Capri, who was an infant. We had sufficient food and water for the day. I knew how far it was to each water station, and we were prepared.

We had not gone one mile into the canyon when a ranger stopped me and asked where I was planning on going, and looked at little Dacia as she did so. I told her that we were all going to Indian Gardens for the day, and that we would return before dark. She then expressed concern that Dacia would need to be carried out. I told her that I was prepared to carry Dacia if I needed to, but I was sure that she would do just fine. We then proceeded toward our goal.

We stopped often and enjoyed all the splendor that can only be enjoyed by being below the rim. The further we descended, the more awesome the rim became to us as it towered overhead. We soon became those small people that we had seen from above the day before. All of the kids did very well. Along the way, we encountered another ranger who voiced concerns about Dacia's ability to make the trip. I assured the ranger that Dacia would be fine.

Soon, we were at Indian Gardens eating our lunch with our boots off and our feet in the cool creek. We were tired, and we stayed there at least one hour enjoying the trees that shaded us from the afternoon June sun. We watched the mule riders as they arrived there, and listened as they told horror stories of how their mules had stumbled and almost dumped them into the canyon. They did not look like they were enjoying the canyon nearly as much as we were.

Finally, it was time to head back to the rim. We packed up and headed out. The hike up was not as bad as I had thought it would be. Dacia showed no signs of having any difficulty making the trip back. She had plenty of energy. In fact, at times we had to ask her to slow down or to quiet down. As a precaution, however, I did make sure that we rested often along the way.

We were within 100 yards of making it to the rim when we encountered a lady in tears sitting on a rock. She had a huge backpack and she looked like she had been in the canyon for days. She was sure that she could not make it another step. Just about that time, Dacia came skipping along, as happy as a lark. The lady looked at Dacia and said something like, "Little girl, if you can make it, I can make it too!"

With that, the lady got up and hiked the rest of the way out of the canyon. Later, in the general store, we ran into that lady again. She hurried over to Dacia and gave her a big hug for being her inspiration to finish hiking out of the canyon.

I wish those rangers could have been there to see that.

South Rim To the River and Back

I had a great experience visiting the Grand Canyon with our four youngest kids one time. We hiked all the way to the Colorado River and back to the South Rim. We planned this trip for months ahead of time. The park service sent us a video about safe hiking practices and we all watched it. We learned all we could about hiking in the canyon.

Since we would be camping down below the rim for two nights, we needed some dried food, so we went to the store and everyone picked out his or her favorite. We took it home and prepared it in the same manner that we would on the hike. Everyone got to sample each of the different types of food. Then, we returned to the store and bought enough for the entire trip. The kids were involved in all of the preparations.

During the hike, all of the kids did better than I did. I have some arthritis that decided to act up while we were on the trail. This was not all bad, as the kids got to learn to wait for Dad! Capri wore a special fanny pack that held our camera, and she carried it the entire trip. After hiking for hours, I looked up ahead of me and Dacia was carrying Shayla's pack. She had it mounted on top of her own. Nobody had asked her to do this; she just wanted to take a load off of her younger sister. That sight made my own pack feel much lighter.

We hiked all the way (nine miles) down the first day. It was a hot 110 degrees when we got to the river. Since you do not swim in the Colorado River because it is too dangerous, we just looked at the cold water, and then we hiked across the footbridge to the campground. The next day, we did get to play in the Bright Angel Creek that flows through the campground.

We had some great times that generated some wonderful memories. We carried everything we needed on our backs. Except for extra socks, the only clothes we took were the ones we were wearing. When we wanted to play in the creek, we decided that we could remove our boots and socks and roll up our pant legs. This worked great until Shayla fell into the creek. She was drenched, so we made a plan to let her keep swimming and then when she was done she could use her sheet to wrap up in, Polynesian style, while her clothes dried.

That sounded like such a good idea, that Dacia and Capri decided they could do likewise. Soon, they were all three swimming in the creek with their only clothes on. I took some great pictures of the happy event.

When they finished swimming, they got their sheets and went into the restroom to get out of their wet clothes. It took them a while to get up the courage to venture out of the restroom Polynesian style. Every time they started to make their grand exit, one of them would drop part of her sheet and I could hear them all giggle.

Finally, they appeared, and it was picture time again. They spent the next few hours wrapped up in sheets, acting like they were wearing clothes from Hawaii. There were lots of pictures and much more laughter.

We spent one more night there and then got up early the next day to eat breakfast, break camp, and hike the mile back to the river. When we left the river and started the climb to the top, it was 6:15 a.m. I had been thrilled to have the kids with me at the bottom of one of the Wonders of the World. It made me a very "happy camper."

Somewhere along the trail, I told the kids that I would pay them money for every typed page they produced that described our trip to the river and back. I gave them a deadline and told them I would set the font, page size and line spacing. They were excited for the opportunity and Joyce and I were excited to read about what they got out of the trip.

Later, Joyce helped Shayla by typing as she talked about the trip. One thing she emphasized was that while we were on the trail, she had been asking so many questions that I finally asked her to stop talking and save her breath. Actually, I made the comment to save my *own* breath from having to answer every question she asked!

Trent was a model big brother during our hike as he carried Shayla's pack for quite a while on the way up. There were times when I asked him to give it back to her, just so she could have the experience of carrying it herself.

As we hiked up, we passed Condor Point. We had named this point on the way down because we had seen Condor #22 sitting there by the trail. We got some pictures with the kids standing right next to it, and then another as it spread its huge wings and flew away.

For the entire trip, the three girls had a goal to have their picture taken as they skipped out of the canyon just like Dacia had done ten years earlier. When we got to the top, Joyce was there to take pictures as they skipped, happily posing for the camera.

It was an awesome sight to see the kids ahead of me on the trail and how they helped each other. There were never any contentious words or feelings expressed on the entire trip. They were always cheerful and helpful. In an attempt to break down the huge task of hiking all the way out into smaller, more manageable steps, I set some intermediate goals. After we achieved each one, we focused on the next one. The tactic worked nicely for us all.

Soon, I was calculating how many steps it would be until our next goal. It then dawned on me that we made each goal by progressing one step at a time. Then I thought about life. It too, is much like a hike out of the canyon. In life, we set long range and intermediate goals, and then we progress toward them—one step at a time. We help each other along the way. We find joy in serving others. They were great lessons learned on what otherwise could be described as a hot, dusty hike uphill!

Photo # 20: Four kids on the shore of the Colorado River at the bottom of Grand Canyon.

Photo # 21: Shayla, Capri and Dacia pose in their newly found attire at the bottom of Grand Canyon.

Wagons Ho

In 1997, there was a reenactment of a wagon train across the Western plains that was open to the public. I signed us up, and then I asked Joyce. She was not sure that she really wanted to take our kids and walk or pull a handcart along a dusty trail for a few days in the middle of the summer. I told her that it would be good for us to go so that we could better appreciate how our ancestors crossed the plains. She then said, "these aren't my *ancestors*, these are my *children*". So I threw in a trip to Mt. Rushmore and a couple of nights at Yellowstone after the wagon train. Then, she said, "Okay."

Of course, our trip would be quite different from that of the original wagon train. We drove our van loaded with camping gear to Bayard, Nebraska and met up with the wagon train, which had been in progress for six weeks. We were scheduled to join the group for five days and four nights. Upon our arrival, we ate a nice dinner with about 250 others who were either already on the trip or were just joining the wagon train. Then, we pitched our tents on the high school football field and went to bed. Wakeup call would be at 4:30 a.m.

At the sound of the call, we all got up, got dressed in pioneer period clothing, and broke camp. We put all of our gear in the van and went to eat breakfast. Then, along with horses, mules, wagons, handcarts and walkers—we started the day's journey. It was 23 miles to Scottsbluff.

When we got dressed that June morning, it was rather chilly. So, Tanya put some sweat pants on under her pioneer skirt. We had been following the progress of the wagon train on the Internet for several weeks, and that helped all of us get into the spirit of the occasion. Joyce and all of the girls wore bonnets. The boys and I wore cowboy hats. We followed behind some handcarts and occasionally got to help push or pull one. It was a great experience for all of us. It was quite a sight to see a mile long wagon train, in modern days, following an old pioneer trail across farm fields and along creeks and rivers. Sometimes, we were on the highway. At other times, we were not. Many cheered us on as almost every house we passed had people sitting out front on lawn chairs waiving to us and wishing us well. I don't think that the original pioneers had that kind of support, but it was fun.

Soon, the sun was up and it was getting hot. Poor Tanya was roasting in her sweat pants. Finally, she'd had enough and said that she wanted to take them off. However, there was no place around for privacy. So, we did what the pioneers did. The ladies formed a circle around her with their backs to her. All of the ladies spread their skirts out to conceal her even more, but there was still a gap. A lady in a red skirt noticed and quickly filled in the gap. We didn't know her, but she helped us much in the same way that the original pioneers helped each other walk across the plains. Tanya quickly removed her sweats and felt much cooler.

We hiked for many hours and finally got to a small town that had been planning our arrival for many months. The townspeople had prepared a special meal for all 250 people on the wagon train. They had gone all out, and they did not even know us. By mid-afternoon, the temperature reached 93 degrees, and I teasingly asked Tanya if she wanted her sweats back on. She assured me that she did not.

Shayla was 2 years old at the time, and she walked many miles that day. She was certainly a trooper. There were times when she rode in a wagon or handcart, but she really held her own on the trail.

People were helping each other in many ways. Some sang songs to lift our spirits. Others shared food or water. Once, I looked up and saw the same lady in the red skirt carrying Shayla for a while, without anyone asking her to. I watched my own kids helping each other too, and I noticed them being patient during some rather irritating situations. I watched them sweat, get sun burned, develop blisters, and get sore muscles everywhere. Yet they did not complain. Today, they all speak very highly of the entire event as one they hope to never forget.

As I walked behind the handcart with only Shayla and another little boy in it, I tried to imagine it loaded with all that a family might posses. We had trouble fitting everything into our 15-passenger van for the 12-day trip, yet the pioneers had taken *all* of their earthly belongings with them, as well as enough food for a three-month trip. And they carried it all in a handcart. We learned a whole new respect for the pioneers and all that they did.

We had police, sheriff and ranger escorts on the entire trip. And when we were on a highway, they blocked traffic for us. They could not, however, stop the trains and planes for us. At one point, we had to stop for a train to cross. As it zoomed by, a jetliner flew overhead. I had quite the view of a westbound handcart and two other modes of westbound transportation that I often take for granted. How the pioneers would have loved to travel on a plane or train! Just the week before, I had been annoyed because my plane from Washington D.C. to Utah was 20 minutes late! This taught me a whole new prospective, and it gave me a new appreciation for the conveniences we enjoy today.

We also had support motor homes with us on the trip. They had gone ahead of the rest of us and we never saw them on the trail. Because the horse-drawn wagons traveled much faster than the handcarts, they too were far ahead of us. There was a very touching moment when our handcarts finally caught up with the rest of the group just in time for the lunch break. All of the people who had been with the motor homes and wagons ran out to clap for us. They knew that we'd had a really hard walk that day, and it was only half over. Deep down, I was clapping for the real handcart pioneers who had walked where we just had 150 years earlier. I'm sure that we still have no idea how much they suffered.

There were lots of pictures taken that day by everyone, including the media. The day started with a man from the L.A. Times taking Carmin's and Shayla's picture. Then he walked with them and got to know our family a little better. The picture later wound up being published in the paper, along with our names and hometown.

The next few days were as authentic as possible, and soon I had convinced myself that I was on a real wagon train. We saw a horse throw its rider. And as the injured man lay there with his young son waiting for an ambulance, the wagon train had to move on. This is not unlike in days of old where people stayed behind to help loved ones who had fallen. Far too often, they had to bury them. This modern day wagon train was fortunate that on the entire 1,100-mile trip, which took over three months to complete, nobody died. There were some illnesses and injuries, but we heard that all recovered.

The last day that we were on the wagon train, it rained a lot. The trail got muddy and some of our family sought the shelter of a covered wagon. However, Carmin was a real trooper and pushed a handcart through all the mud. She was actually glad for that opportunity.

The rest of the trip was very fulfilling. When we returned home, Joyce could not stop talking about how wonderful it had been. The only regret was that we had not signed up to go the entire 1,100 miles. It did teach us many things, not the least of which was to appreciate what we have in our lives today that we previously took for granted. We also gained a much greater appreciation for those who have gone before us. But one of the most important things we came to realize was that learning the experiences of past generations and applying what we learn to our present situation helps us in raising the next generation.

Photo # 22: Modern day kids having a pioneer day experience pulling a handcart.

Halley's Comet

I had waited for as long as I could remember for the time when Halley's Comet would return close enough to the earth that it could be seen with the naked eye. It was supposed to come back in the winter of 1986. As the years passed, I wondered where I would be and if there would be cloud cover that would prevent me from seeing it.

As the time approached, the scientists were advising everyone that the best place to see it would be in the southern hemisphere and in the southern part of the US. Great, we were living in Arizona. I would be ready!

As the time drew near for the comet to arrive, there were articles and news reports in the media every day. We taught our kids about the comet and how rarely it visits earth, and they really looked forward to seeing it.

However, in the fall of 1985, I had taken a consulting job in Naperville, Illinois. That meant that we would be way north of the best viewing area. Since we lived in a fairly big town that was a suburb of Chicago, I knew that even if there were no clouds, the lights from the city would wash out the view of the comet. So, I made a plan. Joyce just turned her head and said, "Okay."

We told the kids about the plan and they were very excited. On the best night to view the comet, we all went to bed early. We planned to get up very early the next morning. However, the neighbor's car alarm went off and blared all night long, so we hardly got any sleep. I got the family up at 1:00 a.m. and we drove south on the freeway for about 100 miles. My goal was to get as far south as possible and to escape any cloud cover. We finally pulled off the freeway and wound up on a farm road. It was empty, so I stopped there. The kids had slept all the way, and it was not easy to wake them up to get them out of the car, but we did it.

When we all got out and looked up, we could barely see the comet. We didn't have a telescope or even binoculars. The only lens we had was the telephoto lens on our 35 mm camera. We each took turns looking through the lens. I told them that they needed to pay attention and be sure to see it then, since it wouldn't be back for 76 more years. I told them that I would not be there the next time, but that if they were lucky, they would be. They all *pretended* to look at it, and then we all got back in the van and drove home.

If you ask our kids today if they saw Halley's Comet, they will tell you that I told them they saw it, but they don't remember seeing it. I hope they're more awake the next time it visits earth. As for me, I will be sleeping then.

Chapter 7—Service & Sharing

Selfishness is an undesirable trait. Everything else falls under the topics of service and sharing. Science cannot explain how a person gains or grows by serving and sharing. But we don't need to wait for someone in a lab coat to explain why this is so. Instead, we just need to start trying to serve others as often as we can. Kids (and adults) feel great when they do. Sharing is a choice that we make to distribute part of what we have with others. The bonding that results far outweighs the material loss of doing without.

Peanuts Are For Sharing

As I have traveled over the years, it seems like I always get offered some peanuts on each flight. When Dionne was a toddler, I decided to bring home a bag of peanuts from my flight and give them to her. I told her that I had a very special surprise for her. She was excited to receive the bag of peanuts. However, I told her that she would need to give one peanut to each member of the family before she could eat one herself. This process of sharing would repeat until all the peanuts were gone. It was very important that she take one last, after everyone else had received one. You should see the joy on the face of a young child that passes peanuts out to everyone else and then gets the last one. I have done this with all ten of the kids and I look forward to being able to carry on the tradition with my grandchildren.

One day, an excited young child ran to her older sibling to give them a peanut. The older one declined, saying they did not want one. This broke the younger one's heart. When I found out, I went to that older sibling and explained that even if the peanut were not desired, it was very important to accept it, to thank the gift giver for it, and to not deny her the blessings of learning to share.

Sharing is a two-way street, and sometimes we forget to be good recipients. My point was well taken and a humble older sibling went to the young one and was suddenly very excited to receive a treat. A good life is the summation of many smaller good experiences like this one.

Service–The Best Foundation

In our home, we have not only emphasized many ways in which the kids can learn to earn money, but we have also gone out of our way to teach them how to serve their fellow man. This kind of teaching can best be "shown," not "told." That means that we, as parents, need to get down and roll up our sleeves and serve our fellow man with our children.

Throughout our married life, the opportunity has often come to us to help someone move somewhere. We have tried to always make ourselves available to assist in whatever capacity we can. We have even purchased a set of dollies to help us help others. Over the years, as the phone would ring inviting us to come help someone move, we would accept and then turn to the kids and see who was available to help also. We have moved lots of people—from a small family of one on a nice warm Arizona winter day, to a dentist with a large family on a long hot Arizona summer day!

On one occasion, we agreed to help a family of six move. It was a complicated move because there were three different locations from which the goods would be moved across town to their new home. I took Monica, Tanya, Blake, Trent, and the two dollies and we headed out. We were the first ones to arrive at 7:00 a.m. sharp, as requested. The rental house had a basement, and the family had stored many unopened boxes of belongings in the crawl space between the basement and the house. Since Trent was the perfect size to fit in that space, he was asked to go retrieve all those boxes. The other three kids would then take them up the stairs and out to the truck. There must have been over 100 boxes in that hole, and the kids worked very hard that day.

Monica had a lucrative babysitting job lined up, so she needed to be back home by 11:00 a.m. We arranged to have Joyce pick her up at 10:00 to take her home. I had given Joyce the address of the house where we would be. In the meantime, our kids got a real good system going and made fun out of extremely hard work.

Before we knew it, 10:00 rolled around, and we started watching for Joyce, but she didn't show up. We tried calling the house but got no answer. Finally, at 11:00 a.m., I got a call from her. She had been all over town looking for us. Apparently the address I had given her was incorrect. Joyce told me that the lady Monica was to baby-sit for had called and cancelled. When I told Monica the news, adding that she could now stay with us throughout the afternoon and evening and help us complete the move, she replied with a response that parents can only dream of. She said, "Good, I am having a great time and I really hated to leave." Money isn't everything!

A Nice Man In A Red Shirt

One year, we went on an extended camping vacation throughout the West. We had been on the road for three weeks. On the last night out, we pulled into Durango, Colorado. We were tired and looking forward to getting home the next day. It was dinnertime and we were all starving. We found a nice family restaurant and went in to eat. When the hostess saw the size of our group (nine in all), she decided to push all of the tables in the middle of the floor together so we could eat with each other.

We enjoyed our meal, but we did feel like we were in sort of a fish bowl, since we were on display in the middle of the dining room. We must have put on quite a show for all the people sitting around the edges of the room. Even though we had been on the road for a long time, the kids were on their best behavior that evening. They laughed and carried on with joy in everything they did and said. It was one of those moments that a parent cherishes.

As the meal was ending, I leaned over to Joyce and whispered that we had better not order desert because of the prices. Besides, we very rarely get desert when we eat out. Just then, the waitress came over and told us that there had been a man in a red shirt sitting in the corner watching us all evening. When he paid his bill, he paid for ice cream sundaes for all nine of us. She said that he was so impressed with the way the kids interacted together that he wanted to thank us.

I was shocked. I asked her where he was so I could thank him. She said that he had left earlier. We explained this to the kids, and to this day, we are thankful to a nice man in a red shirt that we never got to meet.

The Annual Egg Hunt

We have a tradition that we started a few years ago. It occurs every year on the Saturday before Easter. On that day, we make a huge breakfast, invite 250 people, and have a massive egg hunt. Usually about 175-200 people show up. We provide the hot cakes and ask each to bring a food assignment of sausage, orange juice or fruit. We also ask each family to bring at least two dozen plastic eggs and some bags of candy. It is so much fun to see our good neighbors having fun with each other.

While breakfast is being prepared, we have six people stationed full-time at the egg-filling table. These people put candy into all the plastic eggs and put the eggs into huge trash bags. Meanwhile, everyone else is riding the pulley swing, jumping on the trampoline, swinging, making sand castles, playing volleyball, playing basketball, throwing a Frisbee, playing horseshoes, or just visiting with each other.

After a nice filling breakfast, it's time for the egg hunt in the orchard. First, we have the older kids hide the eggs for the younger ones. We ask each child to find only six eggs, take the candy out of the eggs, and then to return the empty plastic eggs to us to refill for the next group.

After all of the little kids have found their eggs, they hide them for the older ones. This is good training for the young ones, since the temptation is always there to sneak some candy. But they seem to avoid it. The older kids are just as competitive in hunting their eggs, and then it's time for the last group: the college kids. They too enjoy the hunt. When everyone has had a turn, we start all over again and keep going until we run out of candy.

This kind of party is not a financial burden on us because we ask everyone to bring their share. And it's fun to hear people talk about coming back the next year. We get our kids in on every phase of the party—from creating and distributing the flyers to cleaning up after the event is over. It shows everyone how much fun can be had by all if everyone pitches in and does their share.

Please and Thank You Game

It is very rewarding to play the "Please and Thank You" game with a young child. Even before a child can talk, he or she can play this game. The entire family sits on the floor in a circle. A person takes an object that is greatly desired, yet is usually off limits to the child. In our home, this is my Cross pen.

One person starts the game by holding the pen. The person on their right then asks for the pen with a "Please" request. The person with the pen then hands it to the person on their right who politely asked for it. The recipient then responds with "Thank You."

The pen travels around the circle in this same manner, and as it comes to a young child, the same thing needs to happen. A very young child may want to keep the pen, but we don't let them. When the person to their right asks for it, we emphasize to the child that the person requesting the pen has said, "Please"—and that we must give them the pen.

After two or three times around the circle, we stop the game, put the pen away, and move on to something else. The next week, we play it again. We have even played it using the same words, but in different languages—like Spanish, Italian, Romanian and American Sign Language.

This game has been a wonderful tool to help teach the concept of sharing. Sometimes, if two kids have been arguing over the possession of an object, I have intervened to play a very rapid version of the "Please and Thank You" game. The object gets passed around so fast that that each child soon forgets who had it first and who it really belongs to! It soon becomes a laughing matter as each is so anxious to get rid of it because the other one said "Please."

Scorpions, Wolves and Eagles

So, what do scorpions, wolves and eagles have in common? Listen up and I'll tell you.

When we lived in Arizona, there was no secret to the fact that our home and property were also home to a lot of scorpions. I killed more than 100 one day in my woodpile alone. After that, no more wood pile! We found the little creatures all over the block fence, in the attic, in the garage, and even in the house. Several of us got stung. Tanya reached into the coat closet for something on the floor and got stung. A visitor in our home put her hand in some water in the kitchen sink and got stung. And as you may recall, Blake was stung out by the trampoline one evening.

I got stung on two different Memorial Day weekends, two years apart. I was in the same place both times: sound asleep in my bed. My body's reaction to a scorpion's sting was worse than it was for everyone else. I became numb and dizzy for a while, but it never lasted long.

Each time someone got stung, we did what we were supposed to do: we called poison control. They were great. They would ask for the symptoms and made sure that there was a healthy adult nearby. They told us how to treat the area and they called us back several times to ask how we felt. If we had gone into convulsions, they would have sent us to the nearest hospital, and then they would have had the antidote flown in if need be. Fortunately, we never had anyone experience any severe reactions.

There was no relief from these pests. We paid good money to an exterminating company who had guaranteed that they could get rid of them. After many months, they gave up and gave our money back. We kept asking around the neighborhood if anyone else was plagued with them, but nobody would admit to having them in their own homes. Oh, they might admit to having seen one or two—but nothing like what we were experiencing!

I was determined to learn all that I could about them so I could get rid of them. I learned that there were 17 different kinds of scorpions in Arizona, and only one of those is deadly. Of all the ones that we had seen, we only encountered three or four different kinds, none of which was of the deadly variety. I also learned that they come out at night and that they love moisture. If you leave a wet rag sitting around overnight, you might find one under it in the morning. They can crawl up walls and even on the ceiling. We got to where every time we went into a room, we immediately scanned the walls and ceiling for these dreaded pests. Life there was uncomfortable, to say the least.

I finally found a company that sold a bug spray they claimed would get rid of the nasty creatures. I got some and it worked! As long as I sprayed every six weeks, we did not have scorpions. I soon became known around the neighborhood as the scorpion expert. I had won the battle with the scorpions!

About this time, Aaron, a young friend of the family, was looking for an Eagle Scout project. I ended up helping him out by teaching a free public seminar on scorpions at the local grade school. The seminar included information on how to get rid of them. The flyers were made and distributed, and then the night finally arrived. I was surprised to see between 75 and 100 of my supposedly "scorpion free" neighbors sitting in the audience! It was a great turn out. I began my talk something like this:

> Friends and neighbors, I am here tonight because I have had scorpions in my home, lots of them. I have learned a lot about them, and I will share that with you tonight. And I suppose that you are here tonight because you just might have scorpions in your home too.

They all silently nodded. I had caught them, but I did not tease them about it. Instead, I taught them.

On another occasion, the neighbor across the street woke up in the middle of the night just in time to see her ewe (mother lamb) being carried over her back fence by a wolf. She called the sheriff and filed a report. Soon, others were having their livestock attacked at night by wolves. There had been sightings of a large male, a female, and a cub. The public was getting very nervous about not just their livestock being in danger, but their kids as well. There were even some men who drove around at night with someone in the back of a pickup truck with a rifle—trying to hunt down the wolves. When I heard that, I decided it was time to take action! I didn't want wolves around my home, but I certainly didn't want anybody shooting a rifle in my neighborhood either!

At that time, Trevor had another friend named Ryan who needed an Eagle Scout project. I suggested to him that he sponsor a free public seminar down at the grade school to educate the public on wolves and what to do about them (or more importantly, what *not* to do about them). He jumped at the chance and put together a great program. It drew 200 interested folks, including our family.

Ryan arranged to have the sheriff attend and explain some of the related laws—in particular, the state's gun laws. He also had people from the Fish and Game Department come and teach us all about the wolf and its lifestyle. In particular, they taught us that there were no longer any wild wolves in Arizona, and that these must have been hybrid wolves that someone had been raising as pets. We even had a group of wolf lovers show up, and Ryan gave them some time on the program to defend the idea of people raising hybrid wolves. It was a great evening of educating the public. We all felt better and safer as we left, mainly because we were now armed with knowledge, instead of guns.

The very next day, as Trevor was walking down our street, he saw the male wolf in a vacant lot. He immediately called me at work. I told him to dial 911 and then to call Ryan to bring his camera. Soon, the sheriff arrived on the scene, as well as someone from the Game and Fish Department. Ryan was there taking pictures and a crowd gathered. The wolf got spooked and ran to another neighbor's yard, three streets away. They managed to corner him there and tranquilize him. Soon, they caught the other two. Ryan had a great story to write for his Eagle Scout project. They had indeed been hybrid wolves that someone had apparently released. No one ever claimed them.

Now, who would have guessed that scorpions, wolves and eagles had anything in common?

Chapter 8—Communication

If everyone in the world could communicate clearly, can you imagine how wonderful life would be? Proper communication skills are taught most effectively in the home. As parents, we need to be as creative as we can to teach kids both sides of proper communication, talking and listening. More than a voice box and ears are involved in good communication. I think that it's called the heart.

Brer Tickle

When Tanya was two years old, her older siblings often overshadowed her. She was the fifth child, and as such, she perhaps often felt lost in the shuffle. She became quiet and shy, and it seemed like she would never speak out. We searched for ways to help her but had not succeeded. About that time, I had to take a job out of town and would only be home on the weekends. This made my time with the kids more important.

So, on one of the trips, I purchased a book and brought it home. When I got home, I gathered all the kids around and told them that this was a special book. I said that they could not read or look at the book without me being present. It was only to be read when I was there to share it with them. The book did not have any real significance as far as teaching lessons, but we treated it as something very special, just because it could only be read by Dad.

The book was "The Stories of Brer Rabbit." It had lots of stories about animals that lived in the woods, and each story had a hand-drawn picture that illustrated the plot of the story. All of the characters in the book had names like Brer Rabbit, Brer Fox, Brer Bear and so on. We discovered that the word "Brer" meant "Brother." We also discovered that these stories were told to the slave children in the South in

America's early years. When I bought the book, I thought it would provide a good set of stories, each with a moral that would teach the kids something. I was wrong.

In each story, we read about characters doing things that we did not want our kids to do. I used these as teaching points. For example, one story had Brer Rabbit tell Brer Fox a lie. After reading that part, I stopped and explained to the kids how we did not ever want to tell a lie, and that Brer Rabbit should not have done that. They always agreed and we would read on.

Each time we read, we would end the session on the floor in a tickling match. That is when I noticed that Tanya was too shy to participate. So, I laid back in the Lazy Boy chair and made up a new rule. The only person allowed to tickle me while I was sleeping was Tanya. I would then pretend to be asleep. At the coaxing of the others, she would eventually come over to tickle me. At first, she would simply touch me and then run away. It was a good start. Soon, we started calling her "Brer Tickle" to make it fit in with our stories.

Permission to tickle Dad anytime, day or night, was granted only to Brer Tickle, and soon, she was coming out of her shell. After a long hard week at work, I loved to take a catnap in the Lazy Boy chair on Sunday afternoons. The other kids would wait until I was asleep with my arms stretched up over my head—and then they would get Tanya to come and tickle me.

At first, it took lots of coaxing to get her to do this, but soon, it became a common occurrence. She would run over and tickle me, waking me out of my much-anticipated nap, but I never got mad. Instead, I would grab her and tickle her. She loved this privilege that no one else was allowed to do. And so, even though she was the fifth child, the others soon looked up to her, and this in turn built up her confidence.

The nickname stuck and she has enjoyed it, even though the thrill of tickling her dad is long gone. Tanya grew up and became a great public speaker and student body leader in high school. We have watched her conduct a meeting of 350 youth and introduce a world famous speaker without reservation.

When she got married, I made a family announcement that the privileges associated with Brer Tickle would now be passed down through all of Tanya's descendants. Tanya's first baby, Mackenzie, died at birth, and she never got the chance to tickle me. However, her younger sister, Janessa, at the age of two months old (and with the help from her Aunt Carmin) tickled me for the first time during a nap on August 5, 2001.

Have I mentioned yet how much fun it is to be trusted with raising our future generations?

Did You Say "Um"?

In public speaking, it is not a good practice to use the word "Um." This word is used as a filler when the speaker is trying to collect his or her thoughts. It can also be a form of stuttering. Either way, it can be annoying to the audience. We decided that if it was not good to use it in public speaking, it was not good to use it any other time.

We had several of our teenage kids running around the house saying "Um" almost every other word. To put a stop to this, we imposed a fine of $0.25 for each use of the word. We got out a milk jug and started putting the money in. The idea was to have a family trip to Baskin Robbins when there was enough money. Soon, every time one of them would speak, they would inevitably use the word. Someone would then ask the famous question, "Did you say Um?" They would then cough up the coins.

As time went on, some of the kids would catch themselves saying the word before anyone else caught them. This led to them saying the phrase, "Not Um," and thus they avoided the penalty. This effort worked to drastically reduce the use of that word in their everyday vocabulary. And perhaps they are all better public speakers because of it.

I'm Tuff

The first time Dionne fell down, we taught her to get up, dust herself off, and say, "My name is Dionne, and I am tuff!" From then on, we taught all of the rest to do the same. This has worked wonderfully. We have even heard a child say it when they thought that nobody else was around. If they are really hurt, you'll know it. But using this approach to overcome the small scrapes and bruises can pay off later in life when the hurt is not caused by a fall, but from something more serious. Life can go on, if we let it.

Matching T-Shirts

We have traveled a lot as a family. To travel with a large family takes, among other things, organization and planning. Over the years, we have discovered that if we all dressed alike, it was easier to keep track of our family while we are touring large public places. So, Joyce made us all matching T-shirts to wear on our trips. Each year, we got new ones.

This worked very well. Everywhere, we would go we would get comments like, "Are you a tour group?" One time, someone asked me, "Are those all your kids?" I replied, "No, we left three of them at home." (It was the truth, since three of our children couldn't go with us that year!)

Another time, we planned an eight-day rapid tour of the history sites in the Eastern US. We went to Washington DC, New York, Gettysburg, Valley Forge, Boston, Niagara Falls, and a few other places. We had to wait three hours to get to the top of the Statue of Liberty. After we spent some precious time up there and took plenty of pictures, we descended the stairs to the lobby. As soon as we were all down, a man came over and said that he recognized the T-shirts and wanted to know if we had been at Arlington National Cemetery near Washington, DC two days earlier. I confirmed that he had probably seen us. Then, Joyce assured him that we had washed the T-shirts in between.

Another year, we all had blue T-shirts with horizontal red and white stripes. There were nine of us and three cousins that went on vacation that year, so we had a dozen people wearing these brightly colored shirts. We got the usual inquiries from people who wanted to know if all of the kids were ours.

Finally, I got a chance for a little harmless payback. I was videotaping the kids as they looked at an exhibit in a museum. There were several of them standing there, all dressed in matching shirts. Suddenly, in the viewfinder, there appeared a stranger wearing the very same color T-shirt. Just as he got right next to our kids, I yelled to him and asked if those were all his kids. He looked at them, then at his T-shirt, then back at them again. He was very shocked and embarrassed—and he quickly moved away.

One time, we had been at Disney World for three days. There were nine of us and we had alternated wearing different sets of matching T-shirts the whole time. It sure made it easier for us to keep track of our kids while we were there. Right after dinner on our last night at Disney World, we decided that Joyce would take the young kids to the van to sleep while the older kids and I stayed until midnight. We split up, and as Joyce and the little ones were walking out of the gate, a security guard came rushing after her and said, "Excuse me, ma'am, you're missing some of your party." She laughed and explained our plan. It taught us that others were watching out for our colored coded family.

Photo # 23: Clifton family in matching T-shirts at Disney World.

Don't Forward That E-mail

One day, I was out of town on a job and I got an e-mail from one of our kids. He had sent the e-mail to all members of my parent's family, as well as all members of Joyce's family. The message contained some jokes, most of which were pretty funny. However, as I read through all of them, I noticed that some jokes contained words that we do not use in our home. I was sure that the child had not written the jokes himself. Upon looking closer at the e-mail, I noticed that it had been forwarded several times, and that the original author was not known to anyone in our family.

This prompted me to develop some guidelines in using e-mail. From then on, in our home, we did not forward e-mails unless we had thoroughly read the contents to make sure that everything in them met our family standards. For the older kids, this only required that they read the e-mail completely and understand it. Since this task may not be possible for a younger child, we asked them to not forward any e-mails at all.

The kinds of emails that we have encouraged are original ones. It is great to see our kids stay in close contact with cousins who live across town or in another state by using original e-mails. Their grandparents really enjoy hearing from them via e-mail as well. But rarely does an e-mail ever get forwarded from our home.

The Hawaiian Tour Group

One summer, a consulting job opportunity took us to Hawaii. We had nine kids at the time, and we all went. We had a great time. I could not find a 15-passenger van to rent, so I had to get creative. I checked the newspapers and found a 15-passenger van for sale. I called and asked the guy if I could rent it for the summer. We worked out a deal and I went to pick it up.

Boy did I get a shock when I saw it! It was canary yellow and it had a huge metal eagle perched on top of the roof! It had been a tour van, and the owner was selling it because he was getting out of the business. We rented it anyway and it served the purpose of transporting us all over the island.

One day, we went to Hanama Bay to go snorkeling. This is a state park that has excellent underwater diving scenery. We knew that the place filled up quickly and that parking would be a problem, so we got there early. We spent a wonderful morning enjoying the plants and animals that live under the sea.

By the time we packed up to leave, the beach was wall-to-wall people. We hiked up to the parking lot and stopped to buy T-shirts as Joyce went on to the van to fix our lunch. We spent about 20 minutes picking out T-shirts for everyone, and just as we finished, Dacia and Capri had to go to the bathroom. Monica took them and the rest of us went to the van. We sat there and waited for Monica and the girls for a while, then I noticed that someone was waiting for our parking place. We decided to start the van and move over by the bathroom to wait for the girls. Finally, they got in and we started our drive up the hill out of the bay area.

Upon reaching the top, there was a man directing traffic into an overflow parking area. He motioned for us to pull over. I told him that we were leaving and not looking for a place to park. He got mad and told me that I was supposed to pull over because the park manager wanted to see me. I parked exactly where he wanted me to and then got out to see what was going on. He told me that the manager would be there shortly, and that I was to wait. Then, he added that the HPD (Honolulu Police Department) was also on their way to talk to me. He concluded by indicating that I was in big trouble.

In a few minutes, the park manager pulled up but did not get out of his vehicle or even talk to me. Instead, he just wrote down my license plate number and blocked my van so I could not leave. Soon, the HPD arrived. They came up to me and requested my driver's license and registration. I gave him the license and as he wrote, our dialog went as follows:

"Arizona, huh?" the officer asked.

"Yep, what have I done wrong?" I replied.

"I need your vehicle registration too."

I went to the van, got the registration, took it back to him and asked again,

Chuck: "What have I done wrong?"

HPD: "You have been accused by the park manager of conducting an illegal tour of youth in the park. I need to know the name of every person in that van."

At this point he was ready to write names as I responded. However, as I was putting my license back in my wallet, I saw my family picture with all 11 of us in it. I said,

Chuck: "That is my family in the van and we are not an illegal tour group. This is our most recent family picture and they are all in the van except the oldest and she flies in next Thursday."

He grabbed the picture and looked closely and for the first time I saw him smile. He said,

HPD: "Wow, look at that family! Excuse me sir, there has been some kind of mistake here and we are very sorry to have inconvenienced you. Have a fun day, you may leave now."

The officer returned the picture and walked over to the park manager and the other man who had been directing traffic. They had not heard any of our discussion. As he told them what the situation was, he was laughing so hard that he couldn't stop. I could see that they, however, were not laughing at all. They looked pretty upset about being wrong.

I got into the van and turned right. We waved as we left. The policeman waved back, but the other two gentlemen did not. After driving a few blocks, we decided that we really wanted to head in the other direction in order to take a different route home. So, I turned the van around and we drove by them again. We saw that the policeman was still laughing, and when he saw us, he waved again and laughed some more. The park employees still did not wave to us. We just laughed and said, "Wait until next week when we return with Dionne and her friend Jane."

The Rules

Before any of our kids owns a pocket or hunting knife, they must first produce a set of "Knife Safety Rules." I have left it up to the child to come up with as many of these as he or she can. The rules are either written or typed, and once completed, they are presented to me. I review them with the child, and if they are complete enough, they can have a knife. If they are missing some important rules that a knife owner should obey, we discuss these and they are added.

We do the same thing with babysitting rules. Before a child can become a paid babysitter, a list of "Babysitting Rules" must be written. In today's world, there are many dangers lurking around the corner in homes where children baby-sit other children, so it's good to put the proper conduct that you expect in writing.

After any set of rules is approved, they are signed by the author and inserted into the child's Book of Remembrance. From time to time, I will review these with the child to make sure they are being followed. If the rules are ever violated, the privilege is taken away.

Similar rules can be adopted for dating, driving, attending parties, and many other such things. It is a good way to communicate with your child and to teach them concepts that you want them to understand. We have found that by letting them come up with the first draft of the rules, we sometimes find things that we might have overlooked ourselves. Letting the child prepare the first draft also allows them to be more expressive and creative in establishing the rules. Setting rules ahead of time, before the child is confronted with an undesirable situation, makes the rules easier to swallow and less threatening.

Smile and Say Cheese

There is no better way to record your family life than to take lots of pictures. Today, there are many inexpensive cameras that do an excellent job of capturing the moment. These come in all sizes and with all kinds of capabilities. An adequate camera is a wise investment for raising a family.

There are 35 mm film cameras that have been around for decades. In that time, they have only gotten smaller and cheaper, yet have more added features. Today, you can buy a camera that has automatic focusing and lighting. Other cameras are digital and provide a long-term solution with lots of editing and storage options. There are also video cameras of every size that record sound in addition to video images.

With all of these choices, there is sure to be something for every budget and level of expertise. Our theory has been to at least record the moment, then worry about doing something with the pictures later. This has paid off as so many of our kids and their spouses love to work at making scrapbooks. And at this stage in their lives, they are very appreciative of all the pictures and videos that we took as they were growing up. We hope that they will do likewise with their own children.

I remember that in 1986, we visited the Statue of Liberty, and I had taken a brand new video camera with us. In those days, there were three major pieces of equipment needed: the camera, which was huge and heavy; a full size VHS tape recorder, which hung from a shoulder strap; and a 27-pound 12-volt battery belt. This provided up to two hours of recording, and it had enough power to start a car! At times, it seemed like it *weighed* as much as a car battery. This camera equipment was much larger, heavier and bulkier than the small, compact, self-contained camcorders of today. However, we are ever so grateful for what we had back then.

As we climbed up the stairs to the top of the Statue of Liberty, the load was not light. However, the pictures that we have of that special moment with the famous lady statue are priceless.

The Polite Soccer Player

When Trevor was a young boy, we were raising him to be a polite young man. When he reached the age of five, he already had four sisters but no brothers. Therefore, he had not experienced all of the rough and tumble situations that a boy raised with brothers might have had. He was not really shy; he was just polite.

The first organized sport he played was soccer. He was a rather large kid, so he may not have been quite as fast as the others. But he was not afraid of the ball hitting him, so he soon became the team's goalie. This worked well for half of the season. Then, I talked to the coach to see if he could put Trevor in another position where he could see more action and get more exercise.

Soon, Trevor was running up and down the field with all the others, chasing the ball and trying his best to kick it. If a boy on the other team got to the ball first, Trevor would simply let him kick the ball. He was too polite on the soccer field.

After that game, we went home and spent some time in the back yard, teaching him that it was okay to not be polite on the soccer field and let the other team get the ball. As long as he obeyed the rules, it was good for his team if he got the ball before an opposing player did. He became a much better soccer player after that.

I had grown up playing sports and did not realize that sometimes you have to actually *teach* someone to be competitive. We did not overemphasize the competition theory, and as a result, Trevor has turned out to be a polite man who has played a lot of competitive sports. There is always a balance.

Chapter 9—Conclusion

Underlying all of the stories in this book is the idea that successful parenting depends on how parents instill certain values into their homes. If we, as parents, do not assume full responsibility and make a determined effort to guide our children, from whom will they learn? I hope that you have found some values and life skills in these stories that you want your kids to learn, and that you will implement them in your own home, in your own way.

The stories in this book have resulted from nearly 30 years of parenting. We have not done all of them all of the time. We do not do all of them now. Different stages of our family have allowed us to implement a variety of styles and activities. Some have worked, some have not, but we keep trying. If Rome was not built in a day, don't expect to raise a family in less than a lifetime.

Every individual is different, and each family situation is unique. I hope that these stories will inspire you to think of your own ideas for use in your own homes. Then, be sure to log on to our website at www.RaisingNextGeneration.com and share some of your good ideas with us. While you're there, browse around and see what we're doing to help others learn more about this important subject.

I have always said that it takes effort to make a family work. Nobody has ever promised otherwise. The example that parents set before their children is more powerful than they can ever imagine. We have found that by jumping in with both feet and trying our hardest, we have had some wonderful results. In our home, we are thankful for the opportunity that we have to be trusted with raising a few members of the next generation.

AFTERWORD

Chuck Clifton is a man who excelled in mathematics and chose it as a major while working on his bachelor degree. It was his goal throughout his education to have perfect scores, and where numbers were concerned, he achieved this goal. He loves mathematics because numbers are so predictable and exact. When I married Chuck, I tried to accommodate my very organized husband, but to be honest, I am not always predictable, and I am seldom exact! Yet, he loves me for who I am.

When parents start multiplying the demands of the personalities of ten children and dividing a parent's time and resources into meeting the needs of that many unique individuals—all realism of exactness and predictability usually goes out the window, but not for this dad.

As each child has entered our family with his or her own personality, it has multiplied our need to be accepting of diversity and uniqueness. For a dad who adores his wife and children, but also needs organization and predictability, he has implemented incentives and directives that have turned some difficult situations into wonderful family events and memories.

Joyce Clifton

Appendix A: Vacation Notebook

When we travel, we keep a Vacation Notebook in the van. This consists of a 3-ring notebook packed full of things we use in the planning, organizing and implementation of a family vacation. It sure makes vacations a lot more fun and relaxing. For your convenience, we have placed some samples of the sections of this notebook on our web site at www.RaisingNextGeneration.com. The various sections and their descriptions are shown below.

Checklists

A one-page personalized checklist is prepared for each person. It includes everything they may need during any trip they may take. They cross off items that do not pertain to the current trip. As each remaining item on the list is packed it is checked off the list. When each child says that they are packed, we review their list. A six-page checklist of family items is also prepared. It includes things such as tents, cooking equipment, lanterns, games, tools, first aid kit, food, and lawn chairs. This takes a lot of thinking out of the packing process. The checklist has saved us from forgetting important things on more than one occasion.

For a sample set of checklists please visit our web site at www.Raising NextGeneration.com.

Itinerary

We make an itinerary, and then make all of the necessary reservations ahead of time. The itinerary includes a daily schedule of where we will travel and where we will stay, as well as a schedule of the meals that we will eat. This allows us to enjoy our vacation much more, since we don't have to constantly worry about "the next meal," or where we'll go next.

For a sample itinerary please visit our web site at www.RaisingNext Generation.com.

Maps

The maps section contains all the maps and any special driving instructions we may need. One person is designated as the Navigator. He or she learns to read a map and how to read mileposts and freeway exit numbers. The navigator helps the driver find our destination and get there safely. He or she also calculates our mileage as a way of practicing math skills, and records this information on a sheet in the notebook. They also record other details. It is their responsibility to keep the driver awake and alert. This provides for some good one-on-one conversation between the Navigator and the driver.

Accommodations

This section contains a form filled out for each place that we will stop for the night. It has a complete record of each reservation. When we get to a motel or a campground, this book is carried in to register and we know exactly what to expect.

For a sample accommodations template please visit our web site at www.RaisingNextGeneration.com.

Journal

Each day, a different person acts as our Scribe. It is their responsibility to record a written account of that day in the journal section of the notebook. When we get home, the Scribes type their notes into a computer file.

This section starts out with blank pieces of paper. When our trip is over, it is filled with wonderful individual descriptions of our vacation.

I-Spy

This section contains a chart of the animal and scenery sightings that is to be part of the I-Spy game. It lists many different things that we might encounter on any trip that we may take. Next to each item is an amount of money that will be paid to the first person each day to see the item. Each person gets a chart. The Accountant is in charge of keeping this section current. The rules of the game are as follows:

On any given day of a family vacation, the first person to see (spy) an item on the chart gets the amount of money indicated next to that item. Once a person has received credit for an item on the chart, he or she is ineligible to receive credit for it again on the same trip. Once an item has been spied on any given day, it cannot be claimed by anyone else on that same day, but it can be spied by someone else on another day of the trip. The person who gets credit for spying the item must say "I-Spy _____" before anyone else. In order to receive credit, they must provide the correct name of the item and someone at least eight years old must verify the sighting.

For a sample I-Spy chart please visit our web site at www.Raising NextGeneration.com.

Accounting

Someone is designated as the Accountant for the trip. He or she keeps a record of all the money earned and spent by each of the children. Each child has a one-page ledger with columns for money coming in, money going out, and a running total. After we return home, the Accountant determines if we owe the kids money that they earned but did not spend.

The skills that the accountant gains during a trip are almost mind boggling, since they are often asked how much someone has available to spend. The Accountant knows that they need to provide accurate information and this requires an organized approach to the problem. This is good training that has paid off.

Knowledge

This section contains flyers and other information on the places we plan to visit. It also contains copies of the Morse Code in plastic inserts. These can then be passed around for the kids to study. If there is a 100 Question Quiz that pertains to this trip, it is also kept in this section.

For a sample of our 100 Question Quizzes please visit our web site at www.RaisingNextGeneration.com.

Addresses

A list of the addresses of family and friends is inserted in this section so that we can drop them a line or pay them a visit while on our trip.

Pens, Pencils and Sheets of Blank Paper

These are added, and in abundance, so that we can write letters while riding, play pen and paper games, record thoughts or creative pieces, or just doodle.

APPENDIX B: DOUBLE A PENNY FOR 30 DAYS

On the next page is an example of how fast money can accumulate. Start by putting a penny in a bucket (better use a big bucket). The next day, put two pennies in the bucket. Each day after that, double the amount put in the prior day. At the end of a month, you will have over $10 million.

Day #	$ Saved Today	Total $ Saved
1	0.01	0.01
2	0.02	0.03
3	0.04	0.07
4	0.08	0.15
5	0.16	0.31
6	0.32	0.63
7	0.64	1.27
8	1.28	2.55
9	2.56	5.11
10	5.12	10.23
11	10.24	20.47
12	20.48	40.95
13	40.96	81.91
14	81.92	163.83
15	163.84	327.67
16	327.68	655.35
17	655.36	1,310.71
18	1,310.72	2,621.43
19	2,621.44	5,242.87

20	5,242.88	10,485.75
21	10,485.76	20,971.51
22	20,971.52	41,943.03
23	41,943.04	83,886.07
24	83,886.08	167,772.15
25	167,772.16	335,544.31
26	335,544.32	671,088.63
27	671,088.64	1,342,177.27
28	1,342,177.28	2,684,354.55
29	2,684,354.56	5,368,709.11
30	5,368,709.12	10,737,418.23

Appendix C: Favorite Family Recipes

Below are a few of our family's favorite recipes. There are times when we need to double or triple a recipe (like pizza dough). We have found that instead of having the cooks do all the arithmetic in their heads, it is better if we have separate recipes for each quantity.

For more recipes please visit our web site at www.RaisingNextGeneration.com.

Frozen Chocolate Chip Cookie Dough

1 lb. butter (softened)
2 cups brown sugar
1 ½ cups sugar

Cream the above ingredients together with mixer. Then add:

3 eggs
2 tsp. vanilla
2 tsp. baking powder
1 tsp. baking soda
2 tsp. salt

Mix all the above ingredients together thoroughly. Stir in the following ingredients one cup at a time:

6 cups flour
4 cups chocolate chips
2 cups pecans

Form dough into 3 long tubular rolls about 2 inches in diameter by 12 inches long. Cover the dough rolls with plastic wrap, place them on a cake pan, and freeze. Frozen cookie dough will last up to three months if wrapped properly.

When you are craving a freshly baked chocolate chip cookie, preheat oven to 350 degrees, cut frozen cookie slices about ¾ inch from a roll, and place them on a greased cookie sheet. Bake 10-12 minutes. They will appear a bit doughy when taken from the oven.

This recipe can also be used to prepare a very large batch of cookies, just omit putting the dough in the freezer. Bake up one or have fun with a ton!

Gorgeous Ice Cream Cake (no baking required)

24 ice cream sandwiches (mint, vanilla or other flavor–alternate layers if you wish)
1 tub (16 ounces) frozen whipped topping, thawed
1 jar (16 ounces) hot fudge ice cream topping
1 cup nuts (optional)

Arrange eight ice cream sandwiches in one direction, cutting some as needed to snuggly fit the width of a 9x13x2 cake pan. Spread 1/3 of the whipped topping over the sandwiches, and then spoon about 1/3 of the fudge topping over this. Sprinkle with ½ of the nuts. Place the second layer of sandwiches going the opposite direction, again cutting as needed to fit them into the pan. Repeat with toppings. Add the last layer of ice cream sandwiches in the opposite direction. Cover with remaining whipped topping. Drizzle the remaining fudge on top for decoration.

This recipe can be made months in advance and frozen to use later. When you take it out of the freezer, let it sit at room temperature 20 minutes before serving. It's so simple you'll feel guilty.

Cream of Broccoli Soup

1 ½ pounds broccoli (cut up)
2 cups water
¾ cup chopped celery
½ cup onion

Cook above ingredients until tender (about 10 minutes), making sure not to overcook them. Do not drain. Then, blend this mixture in a blender until it has reached a uniform consistency

2 Tbs. butter
2 Tbs. flour
2½ cups water

Heat butter in 3-quart saucepan over low heat. Stir in flour. Cook, stirring constantly until mixture is smooth and bubbly. Remove from heat. Stir in 2 ½ cups water and heat to boiling, stirring constantly. Boil and stir one minute.

1 Tbs. chicken bouillon
¾ tsp. salt
1/8 tsp. pepper
½ cup cream (or evaporative milk)

Stir bouillon, salt and pepper into the broccoli mixture. Heat just to boiling. Stir in cream or evaporative milk and heat, but do not boil. Add a cup of grated cheddar cheese to make it rich and even more delicious.

Pizza Crust

1 Tbs. yeast
¼ cup warm water
1 Tbs. sugar

Mix the above ingredients together and let stand 10 minutes.

1 ½ cup hot water
3 Tbs. oil
1 tsp. salt
5 cups flour

Mix the above ingredients together. Let rise to double in bulk, and then roll out onto pizza pans.
Add pizza sauce and other ingredients as desired, such as pepperoni, peppers, olives, sausage, and mozzarella cheese. Bake at 450 degrees for about 15 minutes. Makes 2 medium size pizzas.

Pizza Sauce

1 15 oz. can tomato sauce
2 6 oz. cans tomato paste
1 Tbs. oregano
1 tsp. marjoram
¼ tsp. garlic salt
dash of pepper

Dutch Oven Sweet and Sour Chicken

6 pounds boneless, skinless chicken
1 cup cornstarch
1 cup flour
1 tsp. salt
4 eggs (beaten)

Heat one inch of oil in the Dutch oven. Mix flour, cornstarch and salt together in a plastic bag. Cut chicken into bite size pieces. Dip chicken in beaten egg, and then shake in bag of flour mixture. Place in hot oil to brown, and then remove chicken from Dutch oven.

2 cubes chicken bouillon
2½ cups water
1 ½ cups sugar
1 cup catsup
2 Tbs. soy sauce
½ tsp. salt

Drain oil out of Dutch oven. Mix sauce ingredients together and pour mixture into Dutch oven. Bring to a boil. Place chicken pieces in heated sauce and cover oven. Bake 40 to 60 minutes using about 12 coals on the top and about 10 coals on the bottom. Stir about halfway through baking time and watch carefully toward the end so it won't burn. Serve over rice. Makes about 16 servings.

Lemon Chicken

Marinade 2 lbs of boneless chicken in the following:

¼ cup oil
3 Tbs. lemon juice
1 Tbs. vinegar
2 garlic cloves (minced)
2 tsp. grated lemon peel
1 tsp. salt
½ tsp sugar
¼ tsp oregano
¼ tsp pepper

Marinade 4 hours or overnight. Add zucchinis, onions, or peppers to make it even tastier. This is great to use when cooking on a grill. Serve over brown rice.

APPENDIX D: GLOSSARY

We are members of the Church of Jesus Christ of Latter-day Saints. Some of the terms used in this book may be unfamiliar to those not of our faith. For your convenience, this glossary will explain some of these terms we have used.

72 Hour Emergency Kit

Each member of the family has a special backpack that is filled with supplies that we may need to use in case of an emergency. The kit gets its name from the concept that many times in emergencies, it may take up to 72 hours for rescue teams to reach victims. Therefore, the kits are designed to provide the bare necessities for 72 hours. There are various items of clothing, shelter, light, heat, food and water in each kit. They are all kept together in one location in the house so that if we need them in a hurry, we can find them.

There was a time when the mountain behind us caught on fire and burned thousands of acres in one night. Although we had not yet built our house, our future neighborhood was evacuated at the time. Had we been living there then, we surly would have used our 72 Hour Kits.

Book of Remembrance

This is a set of books that is similar to a scrapbook. Each of the kids has one. Joyce and I have our own as well. It is actually more than a scrapbook because aside from pictures and mementos, it contains stories written by, or about, the person who owns it.

For example, after each of our vacation trips, we type up the journal from the trip and put a copy in each person's Book of Remembrance.

Also, as I have paid each child for his or her good grades, I have never paid until the report card was placed in their Book of Remembrance. That way, when each child grows up, they have all of their report cards available to them. The books are in three ring notebook binders, and each person has several binders.

Family Council

This is a special meeting of all the members of the family. It is held on an "as needed" basis. We have used Family Councils to announce the impending arrival of a new baby, to announce upcoming moving plans, to discuss the Internet and its proper use, to put together our 72 hour emergency kits, to announce a wedding engagement, and many other things.

Home Night

In our home, we have set aside one night a week when we gather as a family and limit our outside responsibilities. We have a special meeting and everyone gets to participate. Sometimes this has been on Mondays, and sometimes it has been on Sundays.

Everyone shares assignments on a rotating basis. Each week, one person acts as the secretary and fills out the agenda and makes all the assignments. One person is asked to conduct the meeting. Another is asked to lead the music. Yet another is asked to play the piano. We open and close each meeting with a hymn and a prayer.

During these Home Nights, we take the opportunity to schedule our upcoming week. With a large family, just scheduling the use of the family automobiles can take a while. We also have a lesson that is taught by a different member of the family each time on a rotating basis. It has been great training for our young kids to teach everyone about subjects that range from how to be kind to someone, to why we don't use drugs. They learn at a very early age to teach in front of a group of people.

We also have a "journal report." In this part of the program, a person will read an entry made in a journal some time in the past. It is very enjoyable to reflect back on our past experiences and relive them again. We then have a "scripture chase" where one will lead a two-minute discussion about a verse or two from the scriptures and how we can apply it to our lives.

Also included on these nights are displays of special talent. This gives someone the chance to perform a talent and to be recognized in front of the entire family. We also always play a game. This is usually a simple game aimed at the younger children. Some popular Home Night games are Simon Says, Down By the Banks, London Bridges, the Please Game, Duck-Duck-Goose and Ring Around the Rosie.

We always conclude Home Night with a treat. They are not always extravagant, but it is fun to sit around and enjoy them as a family.

Mission

In The Church of Jesus Christ of Latter-day Saints, a mission is an opportunity for members of the church to go and explain the teachings of the church to others. It also provides opportunities for service of all kinds to the various cultures of the world. They go to a place somewhere in the world, and if need be, they learn to speak another language. In our family, several have served missions:

Joyce served in Ecuador and spoke Spanish.

Trevor served in Italy and spoke Italian.

Amy served in Italy and spoke Italian.

Matt served in Argentina and spoke Spanish.

Dionne served in Nebraska and Michigan among the deaf people and spoke American Sign Language.

Carmin served in Romania and spoke Romanian.

Logan served in the San Jose area of California among the Vietnamese people and spoke Vietnamese.

Blake is serving in Japan and is speaking Japanese.

When any of these family members has returned from their mission, they have come back better people, full of good experiences that help to prepare them for life.

Sabbath Day

In our home, Sunday is the Sabbath Day, and it is quite different from other days in the week. We go to church, read to our children, hold interviews with our children, write letters and e-mails to family and friends, write in journals, practice music, read good books, organize family pictures, and do other uplifting things. It has been a real blessing in our home to have a "day of rest" once a week.

Tithing

In our church, we are asked to pay 10% of what we earn to the church. In some of the stories in this book, if someone earns some money, tithing may be mentioned just to illustrate what we teach our family. If it is not mentioned, it is not because we didn't pay it, it is just because we did not mention it.

VISIT OUR WEB SITE

www.RaisingNextGeneration.com

We cannot let it all end with this book. The theories, concepts, ideas, ideals, practices, methods and lessons illustrated in *Raising the Next Generation* represent a never ending effort. Through the marvels of the Internet, we are able to connect parents all over the world in one spot to share stories of their own experiences with the rest of us. No two families are the same, and even within a single family, different children can be raised differently. We can all learn from each other! We want to include stories from others in future volumes of *Raising the Next Generation* so feel free to visit our site and share your stories.

We hope that you will frequently visit our website and learn with us as we share information on this most important subject. Then, feel free to contribute to the effort by sharing some of your own experiences.

If you do not have access to the internet, you can write to us to get an application form to be used for submitting your stories. Please do not submit any material via snail mail without first obtaining the proper instructions. We can be reached via snail mail at:

Maple Canyon Co.
PO Box 565
Mapleton UT 84663

0-595-22329-X